# Praise for *Be Brave*

"A book of compassion, faith, and generosity…Florrie Munat helps us understand the complex mixture of heartache and letting go."

—Rebecca Wells, *New York Times* best-selling author
of *Divine Secrets of the Ya-Ya Sisterhood*

"Through the power of story, Florrie Munat beautifully captures one caregiver's experience of what it means to love and lose someone who suffers from dementia. Her compassion, resilience, resourcefulness, and self-awareness are lessons to all of us who walk similar paths. Florrie shows us that generative life stories are characterized by overcoming adversity, connecting with supportive others, and maintaining a belief in the future. Like all exceptional memoirs, *Be Brave* invites us to intimately connect with the author in ways that bring meaning to our own lives."

—Marilyn Price-Mitchell, PhD, developmental psychologist,
author of *Tomorrow's Change Makers*

*Be Brave: A Wife's Journey Through Caregiving* is Florrie Munat's story of struggling with her transition from wife to wifely caregiver as her husband Chuck's dementia progresses. Over five million people in the US suffer from dementia today, and many of their caregivers ride the gamut of emotions—from anger to shock, grief, and anguish. What separates Florrie from the masses is her grace. This grace allows her to move through the challenges and be receptive to the lessons embedded in them. Over time Florrie manages to clear a ground of acceptance and compassion within herself—that allows for times of beauty, humor, and profound love between her and Chuck."

—Corbin Lewars, author of memoirs
*Creating a Life* and *God's Cadillac*

D1400588

"Be prepared for a different kind of love story. In this book Florrie Munat tells multiple stories, each carefully crafted from her attention to detail, feelings, and the ordinary yet significant moments of life well lived. Florrie's perspective exposes her deep inner world of heart-felt presence and reflection, transparent honesty, and humility. The subject of her stories—her lived relationship with her husband Chuck—flows from the beginnings of a love coupled with social justice, through the unusual creation of their family and finally the roller coaster ride of years of intense, unpredictable caregiving and ultimately death. Each of her rich and compelling memories blend into a tapestry that reveals subtle truths regarding the meaning of life lived in love. In her compelling narrative, Florrie brings to light how commitment, respect, acceptance, and kindness for others transforms into the spirituality of miracles, resurrection, and eternal connection. Every page was a delight and treasure."

—Sharon Stanley, PhD,
psychotherapist specializing in grief, loss, and trauma

"A widow details her husband's final years—when he was in a nursing home—but also presents a sweeping view of their four decades together…. Munat provides a clear sense of marriage as an ongoing passage, along with chronicling her separate caregiving journey…Visiting Chuck nearly every day for six years was a drain but also a labor of love. 'Illness could not take away what we'd always had: an abiding love and respect for each other,' she writes. 'And that kind of love does not come to an end.'

A beautiful, richly panoramic book that should reassure caregivers and delight memoir readers."

—*Kirkus Reviews*

# Be Brave

# Be Brave

---

## A Wife's Journey
## Through Caregiving

*Florrie Munat*

Fantail Publishing LLC

Published by Fantail Publishing LLC.
Front cover art from Adobe Stock. Back cover author photo by Rebecca Danon.
Title page photo by the *Marlborough Express* (New Zealand), 1990.
Cover and interior book design by Mi Ae Lipe, What Now Design.

Photo credits: The Munat family (throughout book unless otherwise noted); *Marlborough* (New Zealand) *Express* (title page and page 135); *Middletown* (Connecticut) *Press* (pages 67 and 134); Cliff DesPeaux (pages 71, 89, 233, 236); Rich Hemmeter (page 177); Brad Watkins (page 183); Wirepec, Adobe Stock (page 187); Pete Scanlon (page 197); Thomas Meneguin, Wikimedia (page 204); Elena Kovaleva, Adobe Stock (page 225); Mi Ae Lipe (page 230); Heather Weldon (page 231).

Printed in the United States of America.

To contact the author or order additional copies:
**www.FlorrieMunat.com**
**florrie@florriemunat.com**

First Edition, 2017
ISBN-13: 978-0-9990092-0-8
Library of Congress Control Number: 2017908663

This book is dedicated to all the caregivers
who are now or ever have been engaged in the
difficult and blessed work of caring for a loved one—
and for all the loved ones too.

*Peace and love,*
*Chuck & Florrie*

Where there is great love, there are always miracles.

*—Willa Cather—*
Death Comes for the Archbishop

# Contents

# Prologue

## Chuck's Bravery

*Chicago, Illinois*
*October 14, 1968*

Violence threatened to erupt on South Blackstone Avenue. About forty students, most of them African American, occupied the street in front of their dilapidated school building. They stood quietly, holding hand-lettered signs: "IMPROVE OUR SCHOOLS NOW," "MORE BLACK TEACHERS," and "WE DESERVE BETTER." At the end of the block waited a phalanx of blue-helmeted Chicago policemen in full riot gear.

Peering down from her second-story office window, Principal Monica Molloy grabbed the PA system microphone and barked into it, "Attention, faculty! You must remain inside the building. Police will maintain order during the demonstration. I repeat: Faculty, you are *forbidden* to leave the building!"

Her announcement startled teachers and students in every class-room, including Mobile Unit 409 where Chuck Munat was teaching *Julius Caesar* to his sophomore English class. Chuck knew about the citywide protests over poor conditions in black schools, but he didn't realize that some of his students had planned to demonstrate today.

However, he understood their reasons. For starters, he taught his classes in a mobile unit, which was the Chicago school district's answer to overcrowded schools—a response many thought vastly inadequate. The mobile units had been dubbed "Willis Wagons" after School Superintendent Benjamin Willis, a crony of powerful Chicago mayor Richard J. Daley.

*Chuck outside his mobile unit classroom.*

Chuck was a dedicated civil rights activist. In 1963, he had joined 250,000 white and black Americans at the March on Washington for Jobs and Freedom—one of the largest political rallies ever held in the United States. Standing in a sea of people between the Lincoln Memorial and the Washington Monument, Chuck and his African American friend Leon heard Martin Luther King Jr. deliver his "I Have a Dream" speech.

Dr. King later published a letter in a Chicago newspaper documenting that the city spent $366 per year on every white student, but only $266 on every black student—while white suburbs spent upwards of $900 per student. Having attended Chicago public schools himself, Chuck knew that black schools did not offer equal educational opportunities—one reason he chose to teach in predominantly black neighborhoods.

Only six weeks earlier during the 1968 Democratic National Convention in Chicago, Chuck had been maced by a policeman after he attended a rally in Grant Park. Armed police, ordered into action by

Mayor Daley, had stormed the peaceful rally and attacked demonstrators with batons. *Newsweek* called the violence "The Battle of Chicago" and reported that 23,000 police and Illinois National Guardsmen had squared off against 10,000 civilians, one hundred of whom had to be hospitalized.

So Chuck was well aware of the potential for violence when police and protesters mixed. As soon as he heard Principal Molloy's announcement that police were outside his school, he knew his students were in danger.

Chuck turned to his practice teacher. "Miss Howe, would you take over?" He strode to the rear of the classroom and burst through the door out onto Blackstone Avenue where his colleague Jim joined him. Neither man had any qualms about ignoring Principal Molloy's order. Just then the students began marching toward the police, waving their signs and chanting, "We WANT! Better schools! We WANT! Better schools!"

Chuck and Jim planted themselves between the two groups, telling the police, "Wait, please wait. Just give us a few minutes," while urging the students to "Be cool, don't give them a reason." When they saw the police were not advancing, Chuck and Jim gravitated toward the students. The men reasoned with the kids, saying that if the protest turned violent it would undermine their cause. The teens, distrustful of police because of past experiences, listened while Chuck and Jim pointed toward the cops—all of them armed with batons and tear gas canisters—and asked the students if they were willing to take the risk. Chuck put his arm around the shoulders of a student leader and addressed him in soft, urgent tones. And slowly, one by one, the students turned toward the school and dropped their signs by the curb. The police captain then ordered his men to stand down and return to the precinct. Chuck and Jim exchanged relieved glances as they headed back to their classrooms.

Chuck was crossing South Blackstone when he noticed two black students still standing on the grassy parkway. "Come on, let's go back inside," he coaxed. One boy glared at him and shouted, "Honky!" He threw a soda can that exploded at Chuck's feet. The other boy scowled and punched his friend in the arm, hard. "Don't you know who that is? That's Mr. Munat. He the Man."

He *was* the Man.

And who was I in this story? I was the practice teacher back in Mobile Unit 409—a twenty-one-year-old college senior trying to make her contribution to the civil rights movement. Although I'd been raised in an affluent, lily-white suburb, my parents had instilled a sense of equality and compassion in my sisters and me. During my formative years, every newspaper I picked up fed me articles on civil rights actions—from Rosa Parks's ride on a segregated bus in Montgomery, Alabama, to the Mississippi Freedom Riders registering black voters in the summer of 1964, to the Chicago race riots following Martin Luther King Jr.'s assassination in April 1968.

*Standing outside Mobile Unit 409, where I was Chuck's practice teacher in the fall of 1968.*

The first time I became consciously aware of racism I was thirteen. Leafing through a copy of my parents' *Time* magazine, I came across an article about a black pilot. Though this man was qualified to fly commercially, he'd been rejected by several major airlines. My confusion as to why the airlines had denied this man a job turned to indignation when their reason for rejecting him sunk in. Later, when my freshman history teacher assigned a paper about the civil rights movement and its attempts to end segregation, I wrote passionately about the injustice committed against this pilot. Meanwhile in freshman English, I read Harper Lee's *To Kill a Mockingbird*, and when Tom Robinson, a black man, was unjustly convicted of raping a white woman, I vowed to oppose racial inequality wherever I found it. I was going to change the world.

But eight years later, here I was with my long blond hair and my pretty blue suit, attempting to teach Shakespeare to a classroom full of black teenagers. Welcome to the real world, Miss Howe.

That afternoon I sat with Chuck, Jim, and a few other teachers around a table strewn with beer glasses and bowls of nachos at a restaurant called Smedley's. I had seen nothing of the demonstration from the mobile unit, so I was riveted by Chuck's account. When he finished, I said, "Police in riot gear? You could have been hurt!"

He shrugged. "Someone had to do something, and Molloy had washed her hands. I wouldn't be surprised if she was the one who called the police."

"Why would she do that?" I asked.

"She'd think it would make her look bad to have people protesting against her school. You have to stand up against people like that."

*You are brave*, I thought for the first but not the last time.

At thirty-four, Chuck had lived his whole life in Chicago. When he was a child, his newspaper distributor father had not been able to earn enough money to support his family, so they moved frequently. "Staying one step ahead of the bill collectors," as Chuck described it. But like many children who grew up poor during the Depression, Chuck took advantage of his opportunities. He excelled academically and became editor of his high school newspaper. His efforts were rewarded with two college scholarships that provided enough money for tuition. In 1956, shortly after graduating from Chicago's Loyola University, he married Pat Culhane. Chuck and Pat and their three children—Charles, Isabel, and Ben—lived in an apartment near the high school on South Blackstone. But shortly after my practice teaching stint ended, Chuck and Pat decided to divorce, and he moved into a one-room apartment a few blocks away.

Perhaps because he'd grown up poor, Chuck had a keen sense of social justice, which served him well in the Chicago high schools where he'd taught for ten years. He held a respectful disrespect for authority, whether it was the US government drafting young citizens to fight the war in Vietnam, the mayor of Chicago ordering policemen to attack demonstrators, or his high school principal forbidding him to go outside while his students marched into danger. Chuck cared little for the powers that be, instead listening to his conscience and following his principles. No surprise that the first thing I loved about him was his bravery.

As for me, I'd always felt a passion to be of service. I'd been a resident advisor to freshmen in my college dorm; I'd organized some of my classmates to tutor special education students in my college town's elementary schools. But I was also an introvert who lacked self-confidence—often too shy to speak up in class discussions. My inherent honesty and empathy earned the trust of those who became close friends. However, I avoided conflict and bent whichever way the wind blew to make sure I didn't offend people. No one would have called me a boat rocker, and I certainly was not brave. Over the next forty-one years, Chuck would teach me about being brave. And never did I need bravery more than on the morning of June 18, 2003.

# *MY POCKET OF DREAD*

## *June 2003*

# 1

## The Day Everything Changed
### June 18, 2003

After our morning tai chi class at the Senior Center, I climbed the hill to Waterfront Park while Chuck stayed behind to use the restroom. Because we were near the shore of an island in Puget Sound, I could faintly smell the low tide. A lawnmower droned from beyond the playground as I sat down at a picnic table to contemplate the busy day ahead. We would eat lunch at an island restaurant with our daughter Isabel, our daughter-in-law Lillie, and our two small grandchildren who were all visiting from out of town. Afterward, we planned to take the children for a swim at the municipal pool. While Chuck and I had been busy practicing our tai chi poses, Isabel, Lillie, and the children had been playing at the town dock, tossing breadcrumbs to ducks—which Chuck, an avid birdwatcher, had told them would be mallards and maybe an American widgeon or two. The six of us agreed to regroup here at 11:30.

I saw Chuck emerge from the Senior Center and make his way up the path. Thirty-five years had passed since I'd first laid eyes on him in a crowded high school gymnasium on the South Side of Chicago. I spent the next several weeks admiring his teaching skills and the rapport he had with his students. In the fall of 1968, his thick gray hair and beard were neatly trimmed, though back then many people thought anyone with a beard was a radical. His functional wardrobe consisted of black or dark-brown pants, white short-sleeved shirts, and thrift store sport coats. Vigorous and engaging, he had kind hazel eyes, an uninhibited laugh, and a sneeze that could rattle windowpanes. His family scraped by on his teacher's salary, which he supplemented by working as a janitor at a Montessori school to earn his children's tuition there, teaching Saturday morning GED classes, and commuting to the southern edge of Chicago to teach summer school in one of the city's most violent public housing projects.

Today at Waterfront Park, I observed a man in his late sixties, tall but slightly stooped, with a full white beard and thinning white hair worn in a ponytail. Still the independent thinker, still the man who would defend those he loved—including his family and every under-dog he ever met. I knew his faraway smile meant that the world had just offered him another gift, and he was grateful to receive it. Though he had long ago abandoned Catholicism, Chuck saw the world as sac-ramental. A bird, a brook, a baby: they all represented life's abundant blessings. He worshipped the natural world and was a man of peace and love—which was how he always signed his letters: "Peace & love, Chuck."

When someone you love ages, you don't often notice the incre-mental changes the years bring. Watching him walk up the hill that morning, my only thought was, "Here comes Chuck." And I smiled in anticipation of what he would say when he joined me. It was all magnificently normal.

Until I noticed that he was shuffling through the gravel as if his canvas shoes were filled with cement.

My smile faded. *He's kidding around*, I thought. *He never walks like that.* He did have a penchant for clowning—making silly faces to convince our grandkids to eat their broccoli, or telling a joke to defuse an argument. But as I watched him struggle, I felt heat rise up my neck and flood into my cheeks. When he reached the picnic table, he threw himself onto the bench opposite me.

"Why am I having so much trouble walking? I must really be getting old."

Then the right side of his mouth drooped, his eyes rolled, and he leaned back precariously. As I rushed over to steady him, he muttered words I couldn't understand.

Ever since our marriage began thirty-four years ago, I had been concealing a pocket of dread—a secret place in my heart that held the knowledge that I was thirteen years younger than Chuck, and therefore likely to outlive him. I could feel that pocket wriggling open now, spilling its unwelcome thoughts into my consciousness. I looked in the direction of the dock, hoping to spot Isabel and Lillie. But they were nowhere in sight. Lillie was a nurse, and I wanted her opinion. Should I wait? After a few seconds, I took out my cell phone and dialed.

"9-1-1. What is your emergency?"

"I think my husband is having a stroke."

I winced as I spoke those words. Saying them might mean they were true, and I could be wrong. I was not a nurse, after all. I was a wife. When Chuck heard my words, he scoffed. "I feel fine. Nothing's the matter with me."

I wanted to believe that. How could anything be wrong? This could not be the day everything changed—not today. We had plans to eat lunch at the Island Grill and go swimming with our grandchildren!

Two women from our tai chi class walked by, and one murmured to the other, "Is he all right?"

Despite my deep wish to the contrary, a voice inside me whispered, *No. He's not.*

To the dispatcher I said, "I think you'd better send an ambulance."

# False Alarm?

Isabel was strolling through Waterfront Park with Lillie and the children when she heard a siren's "woop!" She later said her first thought was, *Please, let it not be Dad.* Chuck had experienced some serious medical events in the past three years, including a heart attack and prostate surgery, so she knew that her father wasn't invincible.

Lillie saw the worry on Isabel's face, and the women quickly steered the children toward our rendezvous, though one-year-old Sharky and five-year-old Alexandra wanted to stop and examine every dandelion along the way.

By the time they reached us, two EMTs in navy-blue shirts were standing beside Chuck and me at the picnic table. A third squatted by an ambulance speaking into a walkie-talkie.

Lillie, always energetic and friendly, identified herself as an RN and joined the group encircling Chuck. He had regained his balance so I'd stopped bracing his back. He was also speaking coherently, and when an EMT asked him to raise both arms, he did. My dread began to recede into its pocket. Could this be a false alarm, a reprieve?

"We're thinking TIA," one of the medics said to Lillie.

"Me too," said Lillie. To us she explained, "A Transient Ischemic Attack. It's like a little stroke, but it goes away." I took a deep breath and slowly let it out.

"So, sir," said the EMT to Chuck, "would you like us to give you a lift up to the clinic so your doctor can check you out?" The thought of sitting in Dr. Patel's familiar office immediately calmed me. Chuck and I could give up lunch and swimming and go home after he'd been examined.

Chuck nodded. "All right."

Isabel had worked as a 9-1-1 dispatcher and was now an air traffic controller. So she had no trouble making the quick decision that Lillie and the kids would stay at the playground while she and I walked the single block to Dr. Patel's office. We'd almost arrived at the clinic when her cell phone rang. She listened and said, "Okay, we'll come back down."

To me she said, "They changed their minds. They're taking him to the hospital in Seattle. When he tried to walk, his legs collapsed."

Isabel and I hurried back to the ambulance, which now held my husband. After consulting the medics, Lillie and Isabel made some more decisions. I was beginning to feel immense gratitude for their presence. They determined that I would ride in the ambulance with Chuck, and Isabel would follow in her minivan. Lillie would take the children to the beach in her car. I handed her my house key and said, "Sharky and Alex wanted to watch those *Amazing Animals* videos Chuck gave them. And there's leftover pizza in the fridge. But we should be home for dinner." I felt like I was watching myself in a movie, saying sensible, banal things as if nothing out of the ordinary was happening.

The ambulance driver told us that a ferry was leaving for Seattle in twenty minutes, and we'd get priority loading. I stepped into the ambulance. Chuck lay on a gurney wearing the same tan chinos and yellow polo shirt he'd put on in the morning. That seemed wrong, as if a critical shift had occurred and he should be wearing something different now.

A medic sat down next to him, wrapped a blood pressure cuff around Chuck's arm, and jotted notes on a clipboard. I lowered myself onto a jump seat opposite the EMT. I took Chuck's hand and he squeezed mine, as if I were the one in need of comforting. Though silent, he didn't appear to be in pain or agitated, which calmed me a little. The EMT said, "There's not much to do now except monitor him. We've administered an aspirin and his vital signs are normal."

"Aspirin? Is that all you can do?"

"That's the protocol for stroke patients. He's fine now."

That he was "fine" seemed counterintuitive.

Before the driver closed the ambulance door, Lillie leaned in.

Her brown eyes looked grave. "Don't settle for the ER doctor," she instructed me. "Be sure to talk to a neurologist. And ask about drug intervention therapy. Drug intervention therapy, got it?"

I nodded, but I had no idea what she was talking about. I wanted to say to my solid-rock husband, "Did you get that?" But I sensed a shift occurring even then and knew that remembering would be up to me.

As the ambulance pulled away from the curb, I saw Lillie's mournful face through the window and heard her muffled cry, "I'm so sorry!"

It made me wonder if she knew something I didn't.

# 3

## Three Choices

If I had been entertaining any thoughts that Chuck's stroke was simply another medical problem like his mild heart attack, those thoughts flew out the window when the EMTs rushed his gurney into Seattle's Bennett Memorial Hospital and he became the Emergency Room's number one priority.

In 2000 when he had his heart attack, events had unfolded gradually. For three days, Chuck had been remarking about twinges in his chest. On the third afternoon, he stood at the top of our spiral staircase and called down to me in my basement office.

"Florrie, can you come here, please?"

He sounded anxious, so I dashed to the bottom of the stairs. "What's the matter?"

"I think I need to see Dr. Patel."

"Right now?"

"Yes, the pain's not going away." He touched his chest. "I think I better get it checked out."

I tried to climb the staircase calmly, though my pocket of dread had begun to stir. At the top of the stairs we hugged. "Hey, don't worry," I said. "You'll be fine."

I drove him to the clinic, but Dr. Patel was not in his office that day. So Chuck was examined by the Urgent Care doctor, who said she was concerned about his symptoms, especially his clamminess. She ran a blood test that showed he'd had muscle damage, but the test couldn't specify which muscle.

"I'd like you to go to Bennett Hospital in Seattle," she said. "They can administer a more sophisticated test that will show if the damage occurred in your heart. And I'd like you to go by ambulance."

Chuck looked skeptical. "I don't need an ambulance. My wife can drive me."

"All right. But if you're on the ferry in your car, how would you feel if you had a heart attack and your wife was the only one there to help?"

She left the room, giving us a chance to talk. When she returned he said, "I'll take the ambulance."

The hospital's ER doctor thought Chuck's chest pain was caused by digestive problems, but they did administer the more sophisticated blood test. While waiting for the results, Chuck and I discussed what we would do if he had to be admitted. When the blood test revealed that he had in fact had a heart attack, Chuck was scheduled for surgery the next morning. I went home for the night and returned for his angioplasty during which two stents were placed in his arteries. The day after that, he came home to recover and life returned to normal.

I was expecting a similar scenario this time. But when the EMTs bypassed the waiting room and rolled Chuck's gurney into a cubicle where medical staff surrounded us immediately, I knew we were entering new territory. The EMTs helped Chuck into a sitting position on the hospital gurney and left. Isabel and I stood on either side of Chuck as the white-coated ER doctor flipped through Chuck's chart.

He looked at Chuck and asked, "Can you tell me your name, sir?"

Gazing blankly over the doctor's shoulder, Chuck slurred, "Charles Elliot Munat."

The doctor's next question: "And what is today's date?"

Chuck, an ardent genealogist, who always used the day/month/year method of dating, responded in a robotic voice, "15 June 1971."

When the doctor asked him to lift his right arm and leg, those limbs did not move. But he was able to lift his left arm and leg normally. That frightened me, but Chuck seemed unperturbed. "He could lift them when we were at the park," I offered lamely.

The doctor scribbled on his clipboard and addressed Isabel and me. "He has right-side paralysis, which means the stroke is occurring on the left side of his brain." I didn't like his use of the present tense. The right side of Chuck's mouth was drooping again, and when he tried to answer the doctor's next questions, his words were unintelligible. With each new garbled response, my chest tightened and my alarm grew. A nurse helped Chuck lie down on the gurney and pushed him into an adjoining area. She drew a curtain around them, and the smell of alcohol filled the room.

I turned to Isabel. "Didn't Lillie say to ask about some kind of drug therapy?"

As if on cue, two men in white lab coats appeared. The first one said, "I'm Dr. Ross. I'm a neurologist." And the other one said, "I'm also Dr. Ross, but I'm a radiologist." As if their introduction wasn't confusing enough, both men had neatly combed brown hair and were of medium height. And the ER doctor had disappeared. Was this the emergency room or the Theatre of the Absurd?

The doctors took turns bombarding us with rapid bursts of information. They explained the treatment options, saying we needed to choose quickly—because if a blood clot was blocking one of Chuck's cerebral arteries, his brain was being damaged with each passing second. That news ramped up my adrenaline.

They explained that we had three choices. The first was to do nothing: let the aspirin the EMT had administered thin Chuck's blood and hopefully prevent another stroke. The possibility of a second stroke hadn't occurred to me and I wanted to ask about that, but the doctors continued before I could formulate the question.

Our second choice was the only FDA-approved one: the administration of an anti-coagulant medication directly into his arm. The danger of this choice was hemorrhaging. Dr. Ross the neurologist admitted, "I hesitate to recommend this treatment because it could cause serious internal bleeding."

Dr. Ross the radiologist described the third option because if we chose it, he would perform this relatively new procedure. He would thread a catheter through the femoral artery in Chuck's groin—similar to the angioplasty after his heart attack, but into his brain this time. Then Dr. Ross would inject drugs directly into the site of the blood clot. If all went well, the clot would dissolve and normal blood flow would be restored. He said this option was called "endovascular tPA," and it had only been performed thirty-nine times before at Bennett, the only Seattle hospital equipped to do it.

"If it's done early enough, this treatment has the potential to reverse the effects of the stroke," Dr. Ross the neurologist said to us. "Only people who know your husband very well, like you and your daughter, will notice small changes in him afterwards. On the other hand, it *is* delicate surgery. And it carries the risks of any neurological procedure performed under general anesthesia."

The two doctors looked at me expectantly. "If we're going to begin one of the two intravenous treatments, we have a limited time frame," Dr. Ross the neurologist said. "To be effective, it should be done less than four hours after the onset of the stroke. Optimally, less than three hours." He checked his watch. "We're at about two and a half hours now."

Isabel and I looked at each other. What option should we choose? I'd never made a decision of this magnitude, and this one could have lethal consequences for my husband, who at this moment thought we were living in the Nixon era. When we didn't answer, Dr. Ross the neurologist asked, "What does he like to do? Does he work or have hobbies? Play golf? Like to travel?"

"He's a retired teacher and editor," I said. "He spends most of his time now doing genealogical research and writing a family newsletter. I can't imagine he'd be happy if he couldn't do those things. And we do love to travel." I looked at Isabel. "I think he'd want to reverse the effects of the stroke."

Isabel nodded. "I agree. Number three."

"Okay," said Dr. Ross the radiologist. "We'll do a CAT scan and get the OR ready." The Rosses hurried out. From the other side of the curtain Chuck said clearly, "What were you talking about?"

Chuck had always trusted me to be honest, and today would be no different. I pushed aside the curtain and explained the three choices, including the risks of the tPA surgery, but also the possibility of recovery. He said, "I want that one." His affirmation gave me hope that we were still in this together.

"That's what we told the doctors."

An orderly arrived to take Chuck for his CAT scan. I cupped his bearded face in my hands and tried to look confident, or at least loving. "See you soon, honey," I said, and he was wheeled away. The digital clock in the examining room read 2:35. I was exhausted, but this day was only beginning.

# 4

## That's Echolalia

I spent the next four hours flipping through an issue of *Sunset* magazine in the surgery waiting room. Isabel's husband James had joined us, and whenever anyone entered the room, we all glanced up expectantly. When Dr. Ross the radiologist suddenly materialized, all three of us jumped to our feet. Wearing blue scrubs and with his surgical mask now around his neck, Dr. Ross said, "Everything went fine."

My shoulders sagged in relief.

He invited us to follow him into a small room where he showed us Chuck's angiograms. "In this picture you can see the clot in his cranial artery." He pushed a button and a new picture appeared. "And in this one, the clot is gone and we have normal blood flow." He flipped back and forth between the pictures a few times, then stood back and smiled at us. "He's in recovery now. You can see him in a few hours in the CCU."

"Where?" I asked.

"The Critical Care Unit," Dr. Ross said. "The nurse will show you."

With the news of Chuck's successful treatment we were relieved, but his post-stroke future lay ahead so we weren't turning cartwheels just yet.

Dr. Ross added, "If something catastrophic is going to happen, it usually happens in the first twenty-four to forty-eight hours. So you might want to stay close."

*Something catastrophic?* Hadn't we chosen the tPA procedure to avoid catastrophe? Isabel and I retrieved her car from the hospital garage and sped off to the ferry terminal. Back home on the island, we shared the news with Lillie. Then I threw some clothes into a suitcase, rode the next ferry back to Seattle in my minivan, and checked into a hotel that was attached to the hospital. By the time I got back to Bennett Memorial, Chuck had been transferred to the CCU for round-the-clock monitoring. I sat next to his bed and held his hand, but he was sedated and not too responsive.

When I left for the night, a nurse handed me a clear plastic bag containing Chuck's urine-soaked tan chinos, yellow polo shirt, and canvas shoes, along with his wristwatch and wallet. I stashed the clothes and shoes in my hotel room closet, put his wallet in my purse, and strapped his watch around my wrist. Now that I was alone in my hotel room, I began to worry about tomorrow and beyond. Even though I was exhausted, anxious thoughts spun around my mind for a long time before I fell asleep.

Isabel had been keeping her brothers—Charles, Ben, and Ted— in the loop by phone. The next morning Charles and his wife Hnoi, who lived in Seattle, arrived at the CCU. Ben was on his way up from Olympia with his wife Kate, and Ted (Sharky's father and Lillie's ex-husband) was driving up from Olympia in his car. My anxiety became more manageable as our family gathered, and together we began to absorb the new situation.

For the next three days, we sat in shifts around Chuck's bedside. Nurses came and went from the large room while a boom box played classical music. I spoke to many doctors and therapists. Chuck awoke occasionally and spoke a few words. Always the family man, he seemed pleased to see everyone. But it was difficult to assess how far his recovery had progressed because he slept most of the time.

After three days, the kids' jobs and responsibilities called them home, but they encouraged me to contact them anytime.

The next day, Chuck and I waited several hours for x-rays before he could be moved to the neurology floor. Though he understood he was recovering from surgery, much of what he said that afternoon made little sense. But thankfully nothing catastrophic had happened, so I'd checked out of the hotel.

At 8:00 p.m., as a nurse settled Chuck into his new room on the neurology floor, he asked, "Is your husband always this disoriented?"

I wanted to say, "This is a neurology unit, right? Don't you occasionally get patients who are disoriented?" I fumed over his insensitivity, but said nothing.

I drove to the ferry, happy to be heading home, and hoped that Chuck's recovery would be apparent by the next morning.

When I walked into our house, the phone was ringing. The same neurology nurse was on the line informing me that Chuck was agitated. Could I calm him down?

I answered, "Yes, put him on."

Chuck's voice was weak. "Hel-lo?"

"Hi, Chuck. It's Florrie. How are you?"

"Terrible."

"Why? What's wrong?"

"Well, to begin with, I'm in this cabin."

"Honey, you're not in a cabin. You're in a hospital."

"Where are *you*?"

"I'm at home. I'll see you in the morning."

"Are you coming back?"

"Yes. I will always come back for you."

I took a glass of wine out to the back deck just as our neighbor's lights winked off. I stared into the darkness. During Chuck's recovery from his heart attack and prostate surgery, he and I had discussed his condition and he'd guided me about the next steps. We'd been partners, same as always.

This time it looked as if the decision-making would be up to me— and so far things weren't going very well. I felt so inadequate, as if I were trying to stop an avalanche with my hands. I finished the wine, crawled into my half of the bed, and pulled myself into a tight ball.

In the morning I packed some of Chuck's sweatpants and toiletries in his duffel bag, drove to the ferry terminal, and left my van in the island parking lot. In Seattle, I hiked up the hill to Bennett Memorial, figuring I needed the exercise after so many hours of sitting in hospital rooms. Being active made me feel better. As I walked, I gave thanks that my freelance writing was at a lull and I could devote myself to Chuck's recovery.

A bright-eyed Chuck was sitting up in bed when I entered his room, but after we shared a hug, he looked sad. "I can't remember your name."

"Oh, honey, that's okay."

I thought of Dr. Ross's words about reversing the effects of the stroke. But recovery would take time. So I sat on the bed and tried to discuss our future, but I couldn't understand Chuck's muddled responses. I showed him pictures of our children from my wallet, and although he recognized them, he couldn't remember their names either. Someone had combed his hair into a ponytail but neglected his beard, which held bits of cereal. In the past when I'd pointed out that he had crumbs in his beard, he'd joke, "I'm saving them for later in case I get hungry." But that didn't seem funny at the moment. Since he couldn't hold the brush, I groomed his beard for him.

I suggested we try a few songs. I'd heard that singing and speaking initiated in different parts of the brain, and sometimes even nonverbal stroke patients could sing. We managed to chirp out "You Are My Sunshine" and "Yes, Sir, That's My Baby" when two young women knocked on the door. They introduced themselves as a physical therapist and an occupational therapist. When I admitted I didn't understand the difference, they explained how their jobs varied and complemented each other. They added that they were part of an evaluation team that would decide if Chuck had progressed far enough to transfer into Bennett's rehabilitation unit. If not, the physical therapist said, "He might need to recover at another facility and then transfer back to Bennett for rehab later."

Their vocabulary confused me. I didn't understand what happened in *rehab*, and I'd always thought of *facilities* as gymnasiums or campgrounds or bathrooms (as in: "May I please use the facilities?"). They patiently explained that in their world, "facility" meant a *skilled nursing facility*—or what I would call a nursing home.

Nursing homes I knew. Chuck's mother, who suffered from Parkinson's disease, had resided in a nursing home near us when we lived in Connecticut. Prior to this, she had collapsed onto the floor of her Chicago apartment and lay there overnight until a neighbor found her and phoned Chuck. He flew out the same day and quickly determined that she could no longer live alone. In a week's time, he closed all her accounts, emptied her apartment, arranged to ship her furniture to her grandchildren, and flew back to Connecticut with her in first-class seats. While Chuck was in Chicago, I scoped out nursing homes and chose one near our house. Then I arranged for an ambulance to meet them at the airport and drive her directly there.

For the four years she lived in the nursing home, I visited almost every day, sometimes reading aloud to her; and Chuck saw her each evening on his way home from work even when the classroom newspaper he edited was in the middle of a deadline-heavy publishing year. We celebrated every holiday and family birthday in her room—opening presents and eating cake with Grammy Munat. As family historian, Chuck recorded his mother's memories in a red ledger book with each page representing a year of her life, which had been tragic in many respects. She often said that she was happier in the nursing home than at any other time in her life because everyone was so kind to her. After she died, it took a year before Chuck could say the word "mother" without crying.

After the therapists left Chuck's hospital room, I was grappling with the idea of how a nursing home fit into his recovery plan when the head of Bennett's rehabilitation unit appeared. She was a thin, intense, Chinese American woman in a starched white coat. Health-care workers who treat people with neurological issues often ask their patients a set of questions, such as the Mini-Mental State Exam (MMSE), to assess their level of cognitive impairment. Dr. Chan began her version.

Pencil poised over her clipboard, she asked, "What is your name?"

"Chuck Munat."

"What is your date of birth?"

"25 April 1934."

*Two correct answers!* I began to get excited.

"Who is the president?"

"I don't know his name." [Pause.] "But I don't much like him."

"Do you know where you are?"

"Hospital."

"Do you know what city you're in?"

"Chicago."

"You're in Bennett Memorial Hospital in Seattle."

Chuck repeated, "Bennett Memorial Hospital in Seattle."

Dr. Chan turned to me. "You see he can repeat the words if I say them to him."

Chuck looked her in the eye and said, "That's echolalia."

*That's my boy!* Can't remember my name and doesn't know what city he's in, but from God knows what deep recesses of his brain, Chuck managed to pull out the scientific term for the automatic repetition of words spoken by another person. I had to go home and look it up in my dictionary. But apparently he made an impression on Dr. Chan. She lowered her clipboard upon Chuck's sesquipedalian statement and said, "You're a pretty smart guy."

He was moved to Bennett's rehab floor the following Monday for an anticipated three-week stay. So no nursing home! Excuse me. I mean, no skilled nursing facility. Whatever, it seemed like we'd taken a step forward.

# 5

# Always Young in Our Hearts

Does it seem strange to you that even as a newlywed I held a secret pocket of dread about Chuck's death? Being thirteen years younger played a part, and he and I had discussed the likelihood that he would die first. But long before I met Chuck, I learned that death can come for anyone, anytime. Not just elderly grandparents. Anyone.

As the youngest of four daughters, my only chance to have a little brother or sister occurred when my two older sisters Susie and Barbie had children of their own. The age gap between my two siblings and me was large: twelve and thirteen years. By the time I entered first grade, they'd already left home to attend Cornell University, and then they both married and moved to Massachusetts. I only saw their families once or twice a year.

But when I was ten, Barbie brought her two children back home to live with us for six months. Little Jerry was three, and baby Peggy was just one month old. I was thrilled!

Little Jerry always made us giggle at the dinner table when we sang the line from our traditional grace, "Be here and everywhere adored." Jerry would wait for the only word he thought he understood and then yell out, "Door!"

My father called Peggy an "angel baby" because she almost never cried. Every morning when he crept into her nursery, he would find her twirling a little red doll over her head. Dad would say, "Our girls cried and wanted to be fed when they woke up. But Peggy just plays by herself until someone comes to get her."

I carried Peggy around, helped Barbie give her baths, and showed her off to my friends. I couldn't wait to get home from school because when Peggy saw me, she would smile and kick her little feet in excitement. I was heartbroken when she and Barbie and Little Jerry left us to return to Massachusetts.

One morning about three months later, my father came into my room to wake me for school. Everything was familiar: the way he pulled up the window shades allowing the room to fill with spring sunshine, the way the blue jays were squawking in the oak tree outside my window, the way my school clothes were laid out on my chair. Everything was familiar except his words: "Yesterday something very sad happened."

*My baby niece Peggy and me in 1957.*

He told me that Peggy had been unable to stop crying, so Barbie took her to the doctor. The doctor said Peggy had a telescoped intestine and needed emergency surgery.

"They thought they could fix it," said Dad. "But before they could start the surgery, Peggy died on the operating table."

He patted my leg and went downstairs for breakfast.

I lay in bed and counted the months that Peggy had been alive. Ten. The one thing I couldn't understand was why the sun was still shining when the universe had so obviously shifted.

My third sister Carol was nearly six years older than I, which was also a pretty big age gap. During most of my early life we hardly noticed each other. But when I was about ten, our lives began to dovetail as I became interested in everything she was doing. I developed special pride in her accomplishments in dance and theater. By the time I entered junior high school, Carol and I had become great pals. We played piano duets together—she wearing her Snoopy "To Dance Is To Live!" sweatshirt— and we'd collapse with laughter when I played a wrong note.

Much to our mother's chagrin, Carol taught me how to put on eye makeup and shave my legs. She invited me to sit on her bed while she played record albums like *West Side Story* and *The Pajama Game*, and I would sing along to "I Like to Be in America!" and "Hernando's Hideaway" while she danced in her underwear.

When Carol became the darling of the high school music department, I was her staunchest fan. One night I sat spellbound in the high school auditorium during the performance of Carol's original composition, "Caliban in the Mines," based on a poem by Louis Untermeyer and featuring two pianos and a 750-voice choir. When Carol's music crescendoed to high C and ended with a flourish, I jumped to my feet and clapped until my hands turned bright red.

At Northwestern University, she continued to receive high praise for her choreography and theater directing. She performed in summer stock in Pennsylvania and seemed poised for a career in theater. In December 1965, right after her graduation, Carol and a classmate bought a theater school in San Francisco and moved to the West Coast. But by the following summer, the school was struggling financially and her partner had bailed. Desperate to find financial backing for the school, Carol reached out to several philanthropists, but none of them offered to help. She took a day job at an insurance company to pay her bills while continuing to teach acting classes at night. She was burning her candle at both ends.

That same summer of 1966, she met the French mime Marcel Marceau while he was in San Francisco on tour. The two of them spent many hours discussing physical characterization, a subject dear to both their hearts.

In September, Carol called home and admitted that she was terribly lonely and missed her family. So Mom and Dad paid my airfare to San Francisco where Carol and I spent a week together before my sophomore year of college.

*My older sister Carol.*

Our time was filled with visits to Chinatown where we bought rum-flavored mooncakes and ate them watching the late show; drives across the Golden Gate Bridge while she cursed her business partner, and where we once stopped to throw her wedding ring into San Francisco Bay (she'd married at nineteen, divorced at twenty-one); beyond-our-means steak dinners in Sausalito; after-theater chats with summer stock actors; long, into-the-night conversations with Larry, her pianist friend, whom we afterward dropped off downtown near the gay bars. And runs for cable cars that never waited.

The time I remember most clearly is our last night together. Though the temperature had dropped to forty degrees, we put down the top of her Corvair convertible and plunged through the fog up a winding road to the top of Twin Peaks. Our parents would never have done this sort of crazy thing, which was probably why it appealed to me. With the top down and the heater running full blast, we watched the fog roll in from the Pacific and spread across the city, extinguishing all but a few of the lights. Then the fog passed on, Market Street lit up again, and San Francisco became visible once more. But then another blanket of fog rolled in and the city disappeared again. We watched in silence as the process repeated itself over and over.

At one point the fog grew so thick it seemed that all the lights would disappear, creating utter blackness. We both involuntarily leaned forward in our seats, straining to see. But just as the last tiny light was about to be extinguished, the fog passed on, the city lights returned, and we sat back. I remember thinking that must be what death was like—to sit powerless while all the lights you could see were snuffed out one by one.

After I returned to college in small-town Wisconsin, Carol and San Francisco lingered in my mind. She had suggested I transfer to San Francisco State, and even said I could share her apartment.

In early November my parents called to tell me that the night before, Carol had walked forty blocks from her apartment near Golden Gate Park all the way to Ocean Beach. She sat on the sand in the dark and watched the waves and then walked forty blocks back home. After her long hike, she threw some clothes in a suitcase and caught a red-eye flight from San Francisco to Chicago that arrived at 6:00 a.m. When my father put Carol on the phone, I didn't ask about her beach walk; instead I cheerfully told her I'd see her at Thanksgiving. She told me that she'd made an appointment with her psychiatrist in Evanston. I didn't know she *had* a psychiatrist in Evanston.

Two weeks later, my parents called again to say that Carol had stayed up late one night and caught a bad cold. The cold had turned into pneumonia, and when Carol became delirious with fever, Mom and Dad had her admitted to the hospital. In a way, I was relieved. Carol had been overworked and overtired ever since she moved to California. Now she would be forced to get some rest. Once she recovered, I had no doubt she would go back to San Francisco and start dancing and teaching again.

When I arrived home for Thanksgiving break, the first thing I did was buy Carol a birthday present: a vinyl record of Ralph Vaughan Williams's *Fantasia on a Theme by Thomas Tallis*—a beautiful piece I thought she would love. I still have it. Carol died the Tuesday before Thanksgiving—the day after her twenty-fifth birthday—at Evanston Hospital, the same hospital where she and I had been born. Her funeral was held the day after Thanksgiving. The following Sunday I returned to Wisconsin to finish the fall term and take final exams. Everything was a blur; I got straight A's.

Between Christmas and New Year's, my mother and father and I flew to San Francisco to empty her apartment, see her friends and theater colleagues, and begin our grieving in a very concrete way. My parents were wise to know we needed to do this together. On our last day, I drove Carol's Corvair to the top of Twin Peaks on a clear, bright afternoon. The buildings of downtown shimmered in the distance, and close by I could see every small window in every building, so unlike our night in the fog. Everything looked so stable and permanent. But I no longer trusted stability and permanence.

Two years after Carol died, I arranged to meet Marcel Marceau following his two-hour solo performance at the University of Wisconsin. I waited backstage for twenty minutes with the smell of sawdust hanging in the air as workers struck the set. Suddenly the world-famous mime appeared before me, sans makeup and wearing a white shirt and gray pants with suspenders. Gazing into my eyes, he said, "Please tell me what happened, whatever you can remember about Carol's death."

I related the story of her last days as best as I could, and then M. Marceau gently placed his hands on my shoulders and kissed me on both cheeks. "Now," he said, "she will always be young in our hearts."

One of the greatest sorrows in my life is that Carol and Chuck never met. How can that be, given that I love them both so much? But Carol greased the rails for me to accept and love Chuck. Had she not courageously pursued her theatrical career and maverick style of living, I would never have had the courage to choose Chuck—an older, liberal, maverick sort of guy—as my husband. And so in a way, Carol and Chuck did meet. Not in person, of course. They met in me.

And now, for thirty-five years, Chuck and I had shared a love like the one e.e. cummings described as "the wonder that's keeping the stars apart." I couldn't bear the thought of losing him. But I knew it was possible. Thus, my pocket of dread.

# *THE NEW CHUCK*

## *June–August 2003*

# 6

---

# The Needy Impostor

Chuck did well in the hospital's physical therapy program. Within a week, he had progressed from a walker to a cane to walking unassisted. The PT, a robust African American man named Jackie, followed a sauntering Chuck up and down the hospital corridors and shrugged as if to say, "I have no idea how he's recovering so fast." Watching him walk normally buoyed my spirits enormously and gave me hope for our future.

But Chuck struggled to reclaim his brainpower. Along with physical and occupational therapies, he was also receiving speech therapy. His speech therapist gave him a three-ring binder titled, "Charles Munat *Exercise Workbook*," which is crammed with pages of fill-in-the-blank word exercises and elementary crossword puzzles. About half the puzzle squares are filled with his nearly illegible capital letters; the rest are blank. For the clue, "The opposite of yes," the man who had published a children's book called *26 Challenging Crossword Puzzles*, wrote, "_ O." Chuck had written poetry, most memorably his "Ode to Beer," but now his attempt to solve the clue, "Writer of poems," became "M E _ T."

For one exercise, he was supposed to list three items in each of forty categories. For "Fruits," he wrote, "LEMONS, LIMES." Thirty-eight of the remaining categories are blank, though under the category "Cars," he did write, "LEMONS, LIMES." Well, maybe lemons.

Each day when I entered his hospital room, I longed for his familiar greeting, "Hi, honey." I desperately hoped that the old Chuck would be back. But instead, the new Chuck was there: the wild-eyed one who couldn't name three fruits. In response to the instruction, "Complete each list with a similar item: *monkey, tiger, hippopotamus,* _____" the former English teacher wrote "MAN."

How could this new Chuck be my logical, intelligent husband, who only a few days ago had spent hours filling in genealogical charts and writing his family newsletter, "Us & Our World"? How could this be the same man who last week had driven a car, tied his shoes, taken a shower, done the laundry? He couldn't do any of those things now. Where had my strong, independent husband gone? And who was this needy impostor inhabiting his body?

Questions haunted me: Would he recover? Would the old Chuck ever come back? And if he didn't, then follows an even more tortured question: *Is it my fault?*

Why would I ask myself such a question? Rationally I knew I could not be responsible for Chuck's stroke. But at some deep level I felt I had failed. Perhaps that sense of nurturing one's family—of making sure our husbands and children are cared for—is buried deep in our maternal DNA. Whatever the reason, I felt Chuck's illness was my fault because I had failed to carry out my most fundamental duty: to keep my husband healthy. Claiming responsibility for Chuck's well-being not only presumed I had a lot more power than I had, but it also prevented me from accepting reality—and piled a ton of guilt on my shoulders.

The night I told him he wasn't in a cabin, the neurology nurse came back on the phone and told me that Chuck had calmed down. That night I went to bed thinking, "At least I did *one* thing right."

A week after his tPA surgery, I was pushing Chuck in his wheelchair (hospital regulations) to a therapy session when I saw Dr. Ross the neurologist walking toward us.

He grabbed Chuck's shoulder, but addressed me. "How's our guy?" Then he gushed, "His recovery has been inspirational!"

The day before, Chuck's hospital doctor had brought a group of interns into Chuck's room on the rehab floor. This doctor also used the I-word to describe Chuck's stroke recovery. *Inspirational* was not the adjective I would have chosen, but I wasn't the doctor. Dr. Ross added, "I want to start him on a Parkinson's medication though. He shows definite signs of Parkinson's disease."

Dr. Patel had also noticed Chuck's Parkinson-like symptoms: a shuffling gait, stooped posture, problems sleeping, and lack of facial expression. We had scheduled an appointment with a neurologist to follow up on that possibility, but the stroke happened first. I didn't question these doctors' opinions or the addition of a Parkinson's medication to Chuck's expanding pharmaceutical list.

As his stay in the hospital continued, Chuck did not improve much in either speech or occupational therapies. Still fatigued from the stroke and tPA procedure, he was lulled to sleep during these less active sessions. I wondered if his ability to extricate the word "echolalia" from his brain had unduly impressed Dr. Chan, and maybe he'd been admitted to hospital rehab too soon.

But more disturbing than falling asleep during speech therapy was Chuck's out-of-kilter sense of reality. One night, a hospital aide found him, barefoot and in a hospital gown, wandering around the floor above the rehab unit. Chuck told the aide he wanted to go home. But in his confusion, he rode the elevator up instead of down. In medical parlance, this late-day restlessness is called *sundowning*.

Chuck's problems with swallowing led to choking incidents that left him red-faced and exhausted. After two weeks of physical therapy, he began to lose his balance and had to revert to a walker. He had become dependent on hospital staff for dressing, bathing, and toileting, and he continued to sleep poorly at night and nap during the day.

After his attempt to leave the hospital, a rehab nurse confided in me that Chuck was "shifty," which convinced me that she shouldn't be working with neurology patients.

"You think he's *choosing* to act this way?" I asked her, wishing she could have known him last year—or last month.

But the next day he was moved from a large double room at the end of the hall to a small single directly in front of the nursing station so they could "keep an eye on him," as if he were a naughty child. His new room was cramped, with barely enough room for me to pull up a chair next to his bed. He began agitating about coming home.

"Soon," I said to placate him. "Very soon."

Behind the nursing station hung a whiteboard listing patients' names with the dates they would be discharged from the hospital. When I noticed that Chuck's date was only a few days away, I panicked. How could I take care of him at home? I expressed my fears to the same nurse who had called him shifty.

"The board says July 2 is his discharge date," I told her. "That's too soon."

"Why?"

"He's got ten or fifteen people taking care of him here. At home I'll be all by myself."

"What are we doing here that you can't do at home?"

"Well..." My mind fumbled for an answer. "Thickening his drinks and preparing his pureed foods."

"You've got a blender, don't you?"

Others were more sensitive. I sought out the rehab psychologist and told him I was depressed. It was the first time I had asked for help. We talked, and he told me that my feelings were typical for someone whose life had been turned upside down over the past two weeks. It made me feel a little better to know that my feelings were normal.

A social worker explained to me that Chuck did not have to come straight home from the hospital. He could go to a skilled nursing facility (aka, a nursing home) for more rehabilitation therapy. She offered to work on finding a place for Chuck and suggested I check out some facilities near our home.

This conversation relieved me a great deal, but it presumed that Chuck was going to get better. I remembered what Dr. Ross the neurologist had said to Isabel and me in favor of the tPA treatment. He'd said that Chuck could recover to the point where only people who'd known him well before his stroke could see subtle changes in him. But so far, the deficits in Chuck's cognition were anything but subtle. Even a stranger could take one look at him and know that something was significantly wrong.

Not only did Chuck look distraught and confused, he did not retain any memories of his stroke or the life-altering days that followed.

So he had no idea what his current condition might mean for our future—which I thought about every waking minute.

One day when he was struggling to speak, I asked him, "Don't you feel frustrated when you can't express yourself?"

He shook his head, and these words poured out: "No, I don't feel frustrated. I feel grateful to be alive."

When we were raising our family in Connecticut, Chuck always woke the kids for school with the much-hated chant, "Rise and shine! Rise and shine!" Then, armed with binoculars and a mug of coffee, he would station himself in front of the large living room windows to search for birds among the maples, dogwoods, and birches. Sometimes he would burst into song: "Oh, what a beautiful mornin'! Oh, what a beautiful day!" Despite our kids' complaints that he sang off-key, they later confessed their fondness and gratitude for having a father who expressed his love of life, especially so early in the morning.

I was amazed that from the cavern of his mental confusion Chuck could extract an expression of gratitude about being alive.

But at that moment in my life, being alive meant feeling overwhelmed. And soon it would be time to leave the hospital and begin the next phase of this terrifying journey.

# 7

# My New Insane Routine

On July 4, I awoke to find a phone message that had been left at 12:45 a.m. A hospital nurse said that Chuck was agitated and wanted to talk to me. As I made our usual pot of coffee—which turned out to be more than I could drink by myself—I felt both relieved and guilty that I'd slept through the call. Conflicting emotions were becoming the norm.

Later that morning as I hunted for Chuck's long-term care insurance policy, I felt a full-fledged panic attack coming on as I caught a glimpse of what my future might be like if Chuck didn't recover.

Thankfully, my sister Susie chose that moment to telephone from Massachusetts. I shared my fears with her, and her cheerful voice pulled me back from the abyss.

Then Susie mentioned that a friend of hers had died suddenly the day before. "He was riding his bike in New York City and crashed into the back of a truck. He was killed instantly!" Susie said. "I feel so sorry for his wife. Can you imagine?"

My first thought was, *His wife is lucky.*

Lucky? Well, she doesn't have to live with all the emotions that I do: the guilt and sadness, the confusion and fear. For her, it's over. No critical decisions, no worries over medical bills, no anxiety about caring for her husband, no wondering when he *will* die. Her guy is gone. She knows what happened to him. She can grieve and move on.

Those were my thoughts. You may ask: how could I envy a woman whose husband had just died? Here's my answer: because I longed for the resolution I assumed she had. For me, everything remained unresolved.

After talking to Susie, I drove to an island nursing home called St. Thomas Health & Rehabilitation Center. I walked in unannounced, as some friends had advised me to do. Each time I had to face a new experience like this, I felt totally unprepared and fearful—as if I were plunging off a high dive into a pool with no bottom.

I had considered two other nursing homes as possible rehab places for Chuck. I recalled that the other island facility was dark and depressing, so I ruled it out without even touring it. The second facility was ten miles north across the island's only bridge, where traffic backed up. I phoned an acquaintance, the manager of an *assisted living facility* (more lingo to learn), who rated the off-island facility as superior, but she called St. Thomas "more user friendly" because of its proximity.

"St. Thomas works fine as long as you have a daily advocate," she said. "And I know you'll be there."

That sounded great, but I had no idea what would be required of me as Chuck's daily advocate. I was about to learn.

Entering St. Thomas, the first thing I noticed was the shiny, faux-wood hallway that led from the front door to the nursing station. Golden chandeliers cast a bright light over the hall. My first impression was that it all looked cheesy. But it was clean, and the air smelled fresh.

I walked down the hall and introduced myself to the woman who was sitting at the nursing station. She held out her hand to greet me. "I'm Sharon, the director of nursing."

When she stood, I could see that although she was shorter than I was, she radiated authority—from the confident tone of her voice to her creased gray slacks, white linen shirt, and carefully combed ponytail. She made me feel that I was in good hands, and I was impressed that the director of nursing was working on the Fourth of July.

Sharon gave me a tour of the one-story facility, which had seventy-five beds. We looked at some resident rooms, the therapy area, spa bath, shower room, kitchen, dining room, and laundry. When I asked if they had any vacancies, Sharon said they did. I thought St. Thomas would be a good interim residence for Chuck between the hospital and home. The hospital social worker had estimated that three weeks would be adequate for Chuck's stay at a follow-up facility, so that's what I told Sharon. I was relying on the professionals to guide me through this minefield.

Later, back at Bennett Memorial Hospital, I found Chuck napping in his small room. When I told him that I'd found a place on the island to transfer him after the holiday weekend, he grabbed my arm and pulled me to him for a long hug. I began to feel more hopeful about his recovery.

First we'd get him back to the island, and then we'd get him back home. That was the plan. That had always been the plan.

On Chuck's last day at Bennett Memorial, I wheeled him out onto the hospital's rooftop garden, a pleasant oasis we'd discovered early in his stay. Just three weeks ago, he'd come dangerously close to dying of a stroke. And during the ensuing days I'd witnessed his confusion, belligerence, choking, sundowning, aphasia (loss of ability to speak because of brain damage), and huge changes in his personality and ability to take care of himself.

As we sat in the summer sunshine, Chuck yawned, stretched his arms, and remarked, "This has been a pleasant ten days." As anxious as I felt about our future, I burst out laughing at his blissful amnesia! And wished I could share it.

The next three weeks introduced us to yet another set of unfamiliar routines at the nursing home. But at least I was spared the commute to Seattle every day, and when I asked Chuck if he felt better to be back on the island, he said, "A thousand times better."

His three new therapists—physical, occupational, and speech—were uniformly cheerful, knowledgeable, and positive. They worked Chuck as hard and as fast as he could go. When he'd achieved to the point where he could live at home, he'd be able to continue therapy there as an outpatient. That was the plan.

Chuck settled into his new therapy routine with brave diligence. And I settled into my new, insane routine of spending almost every waking moment with him. I must have thought—if I thought at all—that if *he* had to go through this ordeal, then so did I.

Every day I left the house at 8:00 a.m. with a brown bag lunch, drove the five miles to St. Thomas Health & Rehabilitation Center, and stayed with Chuck for most of the day. To illustrate how absurdly devoted I was, at suppertime I'd bring two dollars to the kitchen staff and have them deliver me a tray of the same dinner Chuck got. If I needed to shop for groceries or have the van's oil changed, I'd leave him for an hour or so while he napped. Otherwise, it was as though I had moved into the nursing home with him.

I simply found it impossible to leave his side. What would I do if I left? Sit at home and worry? And what would *he* do if I weren't there? I'd lost my will to do anything but observe Chuck and go home to sleep.

I'd been an avid reader, but the only document I could concentrate on was my journal, optimistically titled "Chuck's Stroke and Recovery." I read and reread it in an attempt to process our new reality. I longed for the old Chuck, yet clung to the new Chuck because he was all I had.

I felt anxious and alone. Had anyone else in this situation ever felt like this? And if they hadn't, was something wrong with me? A thornier question was brewing that I wouldn't begin to formulate for quite a while: Who was I without Chuck?

At a time when I should have been sharing all these fears, questions, and pending decisions with trusted family members and friends, I isolated myself with Chuck at St. Thomas. I was charting a dangerous course.

# 8

## Us Against the World

I became Chuck's practice teacher in September 1968. Later that fall he and his wife separated, but when he and I met and fell in love, he was still married and the father of three young children. Predictable opposition to our relationship came from many people. In the circle around me, my mother's voice roared the loudest.

During the years before Chuck entered my life, Mom and I had never experienced a serious disagreement. She'd been my moral compass when I was a child, and I could go to her with any schoolyard problem. She made every family birthday and holiday memorable by establishing fun traditions that appealed to the child within her; and she photographed them all with her beloved Zeiss Ikon cameras.

But Mom had trouble during her daughters' teenage years, as each of us went through the age-old process of separating ourselves from our parents. Mom was so dedicated to her "girls" that she couldn't bear to surrender her mother role. Maybe because I was her youngest child, it was harder for her to let me go.

Plus, she'd been in failing health for many years. While I was in high school, she had two heart attacks and was hospitalized for other strange afflictions like encephalitis and delusional behavior. She suffered from chemical and hormonal imbalances that no doctor could fathom or control. She had been a reasonably vigorous woman, but all these assaults on her body had transformed her into a near invalid with mood swings.

Before I met Chuck, Mom told me she'd seen the movie *Guess Who's Coming to Dinner* and she understood what I might ask of her one day. Her implication was that if I brought home a black boyfriend she'd be ready. (Also implied was that he'd better be an awful lot like

Sidney Poitier!). Instead, I brought home a thirty-four-year-old, not-yet-divorced father of three. What movie could have prepared her for that?

My father was a peacemaker. One Saturday afternoon, he made the long trek from the northern suburbs to the South Side to have lunch with Chuck and me at a bar & grill on 58th Street. He had called the meeting and was generous enough to convene on our turf. I see now that Dad was trying to keep the peace between his wife and his daughter. But he had to live with his wife, so ultimately he agreed with Mom: Chuck and I should stop seeing each other.

*I photographed Chuck in Connecticut, 1969.*

From Chuck's standpoint—although Pat had agreed to a divorce and he'd moved out of their apartment—he was not eager to share news about his girlfriend with her or their mutual friends. In the late 1960s, Chuck's illicit relationship with me could be grounds for job dismissal, and Chuck already had an antagonistic relationship with Principal Molloy. So except for telling a few trusted colleagues, he kept our relationship a secret, and I did the same.

After my eight-week practice teaching stint at the high school on South Blackstone, I shifted to another school in the South Shore neighborhood for another eight weeks. Then, exhausted and demoralized, I retreated to my parents' home for the Christmas holidays.

What had I accomplished by my inner-city teaching? I taught *Darkness at Noon* and *Wariner's English Grammar and Composition* to students who dozed through my classes for a variety of tragic reasons that kept them awake at night. I witnessed the expulsion of one of Chuck's at-risk students over nothing more than a residence technicality. In spite of Chuck's efforts to defend the boy, Molloy expelled him and sent the truant officer after him. The boy then spent his days playing basketball at the YMCA, waiting for his sixteenth birthday when he could legally drop out of school.

In short, my teaching had not affected the civil rights movement at all—not one iota. Why had I ever thought it would? Racism and injustice were deeply entrenched in the system. Who was I to change it?

Shortly before Christmas, Chuck drove a U-Haul truck through a blinding snowstorm to Rockford, Illinois, where he helped Pat and the kids move their belongings into her mother's house. Then he said good-bye to his beloved children—Charles (9), Isabel (8), and Ben (3)—and returned to his one-room apartment in Chicago, alone and disconsolate.

Not only had 1968 been hard on us personally, it had been a tragic year for our country, politically and historically. In April when Martin Luther King Jr. was assassinated, Chuck played records of King's speeches in his mobile unit and he and his students wept together. The day in June when I took my Eighteenth-Century English Poetry final exam, my professor informed us of Bobby Kennedy's assassination in Los Angeles—right after he'd won the California primary election.

Our hopes that the progressive Gene McCarthy might become president were dashed when Hubert Humphrey was selected as the Democratic candidate. Chuck said he would be morally compromised if he voted for Humphrey, so he cast his ballot for Dick Gregory—an African American civil rights activist and comedian. In my first presidential election, I voted for Humphrey anyway. But the November election launched the presidency of Republican Richard Nixon, who had vowed to bring "peace with honor" in Vietnam—but we didn't believe him.

On top of all this, Mom and Dad were hounding me to end my three-month relationship with Chuck. My usual default was to make a decision that pleased everybody, but that wasn't going to be possible this time.

So why didn't I give him up? My life would have been so much simpler without the constant stress of fighting with my parents and keeping secrets from my friends.

And why didn't he give me up? He was putting his career at risk and jeopardizing his custody rights.

Chuck and I appeared to be polar opposites. An outspoken extrovert, he grew up poor and now eked out a tough existence in Chicago. A shy introvert, I was a baby boomer who had a worry-free childhood in a wealthy suburb. He was married with three children. I had never even had a serious boyfriend. Chuck spent years teaching in the inner city, trying to convince teenagers they had a future. I followed the civil rights movement on television and in the newspaper. Chuck and his African American friend Leon attended the March on Washington in 1963. Leon was not only a good friend, but he was also the godfather of Chuck's oldest son Charles. I attended an all-white high school and mostly white college; I had no black friends.

So what kept us together? Was it that we both loved folk and classical music, felt a kinship with nature, liked to watch baseball and art house movies, voted Democratic (usually), read novels, and dreamed of traveling? All true, but those commonalities can't explain why we fell in love. So how could we be so sure?

I'd have to say that when we met, we experienced a recognition and attraction that couldn't be denied. As my father would say many years later, "Chuck and Florrie have something special. I can't explain it, but they really have it." It seemed we had no choice but to endure whatever difficulties we faced until we could be married.

In January 1969, my parents drove me back to northern Wisconsin for the winter term of my senior year. I think they harbored the illusion that if they took me 200 miles from Chicago, Chuck would not be able to find me. As we exited the highway near Appleton, my father drove his signature Oldsmobile past snowy fields of dried cornstalks. I rode in the backseat feeling like a child. My mother turned to me. "Do you know what Anna said about you?"

The only Anna I could think of was my grandparents' Polish maid. She lived in a room off the kitchen in their huge apartment in Chicago. I'd always loved its sixth-floor views of Lake Michigan and the Oak Street Beach, and as a child I used to press my cheek against a cold windowpane, straining to catch a glimpse of the elusive Palmolive Beacon, while car headlights bobbed down Lake Shore Drive. I had an image of Anna, wearing a light-gray uniform with a white apron and cap, serving us vegetables from a platter on Thanksgiving. But that couldn't be the person my mother meant.

"Who's Anna?" I said, gazing at the mud-streaked snow.

"Your grandmother's maid," she said, as if I were dim-witted. I dreaded her next words. "Anna said you used to be an angel child. She doesn't understand what happened to you. She says she doesn't know who you are anymore."

I thought, *I don't know who my mother is anymore.*

Earlier in the drive, she'd used another anti-Chuck argument: "You think it's fine now, but wait until he's sixty-five and you're fifty-two." She turned out to be prescient about that one. Chuck was sixty-five when he had his heart attack, so I became his caregiver at fifty-two. But wasn't it strange her scenario assumed that Chuck and I would still be together?

Two days after my parents got me settled at my apartment and drove home, I met Chuck at the Appleton train station, and we spent the weekend together. We shared a pizza and a few beers at The Mark, browsed for books at Conkey's, walked around the snowy campus, and went to a Bergman film that neither of us understood.

I felt guilty about deceiving my parents. But I was protecting them from a truth they did not want to face: they could have driven me across the Arctic Circle in Dad's Oldsmobile; there was no way they could keep Chuck and me apart.

*Chuck photographed me in Wisconsin, 1969.*

For the next six months until I graduated, I rode a Greyhound bus from Appleton to Chicago every weekend to see Chuck. When the bus passed through my hometown, I felt sad about the rift between my parents and me—and I felt guilty about hiding the truth from them. But that didn't stop me.

By the time I arrived in Chicago on Friday night, we only had time to travel back to Chuck's room and go to sleep. On Saturday morning though, we'd get up early to attend Operation Breadbasket meetings at a large church on the South Side. The Southern Christian Leadership Conference (SCLC), a nonviolent organization dedicated to civil rights reform and led by Martin Luther King Jr., founded Operation Breadbasket chapters in several southern cities, including Atlanta. In 1966, Dr. King asked Reverend Jesse Jackson to head up a chapter in Chicago, a city known for its segregated neighborhoods.

Chuck explained Breadbasket's mission to me this way: "A lot of businesses in the ghetto are owned by white people. And when blacks spend money at those businesses, their money doesn't stay in their own neighborhoods. It gets sucked out of the ghettos and into the pockets of wealthy white businessmen who live in the suburbs. And most of those businesses don't hire blacks, or they hire them only for low-wage jobs. This has to change."

At Breadbasket meetings I learned that many of their leaders were clergymen. Their strategy was to work with local companies to educate management about the effects of racial discrimination and paying low wages. Then Breadbasket leaders would help negotiate contracts with these companies that stipulated they hire more black workers. If a business refused, it would be boycotted.

Martin Luther King Jr. had spoken at Chicago's Operation Breadbasket meetings, as had Joe Louis, the much loved African American heavyweight boxing champion. When Chuck and I attended, Jesse Jackson always delivered an impassioned speech. I had never experienced a revival meeting, but these gatherings enlivened me and touched my heart, especially the music. The Breadbasket orchestra and choir played gospel songs like "This Little Light of Mine" and "Amazing Grace." At the end of every meeting, the multiracial audience held hands, swayed, and sang "We Shall Overcome."

If my mother could have seen me, I think she might have ended up in the hospital again—another reason to keep her in the dark about my weekend trips to Chicago.

In those days when it felt like us against the world, Chuck used to say, "It's simple. All we have to do is love each other, get married, and be happy for the rest of our lives." And that's pretty much the way it turned out.

Once we were married and settled in Connecticut, we vowed to make up for the resistance to our union by spending as much time together as possible. Chuck suggested that we not accept any volunteer work unless we did it together. So when he was recruited for the YMCA board and I was asked to serve on an interracial scholarship committee, we each agreed on the condition that our partner could serve also. The nonprofits loved us! Over the years, this solidarity made us a strong couple. But it did not help me become a strong individual.

When Chuck and I joined the AFS International Club, we naturally gravitated toward different responsibilities. As an editor and teacher,

Chuck was adept at front-man duties such as chairing meetings, emceeing fundraisers, and other high-visibility duties. He once lodged a complaint with the national AFS office over a question on the host family application: "Are you willing to host a student of a different race?" Chuck made the case that a family should be willing to host a student of any race. After some hemming and hawing, AFS removed the race question from their application.

I tended to work behind the scenes for the AFS club, doing tasks like writing, phoning, recruiting host families for exchange students, creating slide shows, and making sure everybody was working well together. When people complimented Chuck on his endeavors, they were often unaware of my backstage support, which was fine because I preferred to avoid the limelight.

Later, Chuck led the way as family disciplinarian, especially during the spirited "Family Conferences" he sometimes called at dinnertime. As parents, our personalities fell naturally into the good cop (me), bad cop (him) roles.

However, after Chuck's stroke, I was poorly served by my aversion to front-man tasks. Suddenly my job was to be the decision-maker, question-asker, and confrontational advocate when medical wrongs needed righting. These were *not* my familiar roles, having ceded them to my senior partner for thirty-five years. But now that partner was a cognitively impaired man who insisted that I get him out of "this god-awful nursing home" and bring him back to our house where he belonged.

I alone understood the sacrificial nature of what his demands asked of me. I alone realized that I couldn't rely on his guidance anymore. And I alone was terrified.

The target date for Chuck to come home was three weeks after his admission to St. Thomas. And so, on Monday, July 28, 2003, Chuck came home. That was the plan. That had always been the plan. As they say, "Want to make God laugh? Tell him your plans."

# 9

## The End of My Tether

After three weeks in a Seattle hospital recovering from his stroke and three weeks at St. Thomas Health & Rehab for further recovery, Chuck came home. The following are excerpts from my journal, "Chuck's Stroke and Recovery," hurriedly handwritten during the eleven days I cared for him at our house.

### *Monday, July 28 – Day 41*

*Picked C. up at nursing home at 9:00 a.m. He was ready to leave! Though he had not slept well—again. At home things got busy in a hurry with unpacking, sorting the meds into compartmentalized daily pill containers, making sure C. was okay, cooking lunch (taking his blood sugar and thickening his beverages first). He now needs three or four square meals a day because of his diabetes. He was less coherent, which seems to be the key factor for sending me into feelings of anxiety and being overwhelmed with all the new activities and problems. It's the "I'm in this all alone" feeling. Thank goodness Ted is here until tomorrow.*

*The blue chair in the living room and our bed are both too soft—and difficult for C. to get out of. So he's sitting in his wheelchair in the living room. The master toilet gave him problems so I left him with Ted and drove down to Helpline House to look for another raised toilet seat. The one I brought back doesn't fit our toilet, but there is nothing else for now.*

*After a nap C. insisted that we watch the "Good Will Refuge" channel and insisted that it existed. It's been a hot day and a rocky one for me with all the new labors, but I have to remember this is the first day home.*

**Tuesday, July 29 – Day 42**

Horrible night. I woke at 1:00 a.m. to find him on the floor next to the bed. He'd fallen but he didn't know how. He scraped his cheek and forehead. Said he didn't want to use the portable commode I'd put by the side of the bed unless he was "sick." We switched sides of the bed so he was closer to the toilet, but he continued to be restless. Used the toilet 6-7 times. Because the toilet seat doesn't fit properly, he wet his pajama pants and then after he dressed himself at 5:30, he wet his trousers. I asked him to stay in bed, and he said, "For the rest of my life?" I said, "No, until 7:00 a.m." He couldn't lie still so I didn't sleep either. Finally he got dressed and went into the living room. I tried to let go, to let him be independent no matter the consequences. But I still couldn't sleep. I made him breakfast at 7:00.

His blood sugar was 191, so maybe he's stressed. All the work of meal prep and thickening beverages is time-consuming. It's not the work, it's the stress.

C. took a nap and then he and Ted and I drove down to Fort Ward Park. He walked a bit and then Ted pushed his wheelchair almost to the end of the blacktop and I pushed him back. Ted had checked some websites on stroke and printed out a few things for me and sent links to Charles, Isabel, and Ben along with an email suggesting they all take one day every four weeks to spend with C. to give me a break. C. took another nap this afternoon.

We did a children's US map puzzle—and he answered all my questions correctly about the states. At his computer he deleted a bunch of emails, moved the cursor around, printed something out. I was amazed. So it really is an up-and-down journey. What will tonight bring? Sleep, hopefully.

**Wednesday, July 30 – Day 43**

Another day that could best be described as "nightmarish." C. fell again last night. I was observing his restlessness—he couldn't lie still, got up on numerous occasions to go to the toilet or to walk down the hallway. I didn't feel I could prevent it, and finally I heard a crash in the shower room. He was half-on, half-off the chair and there was a red welt on his arm. He said he'd hit his head, and he pulled the towel bar out of the wall. He finally settled down around 6:45. I slept a little too, but how long can I keep going on so little sleep?

Got a walker from Helpline House, took C. to outpatient therapy at the nursing home. The therapists were concerned about the scrape on his head. Had lots of phone conversations with various doctors' offices. Went to Safeway while C. was doing therapy. Then we drove to Silverdale and bought a VERY firm mattress.

His sleep problems seem to be exacerbating the whole recovery process, yet I don't want to start him on a med to sedate him. Nothing has worked so far, and the mix with what he's already on could make him worse.

I spent a lot of time on the phone trying to sort out his prescription refills with Dr. Chan's office, and finally they informed me that his primary care physician, Dr. Patel, is in charge of his meds. When I called Dr. Patel's office, they told me that he was leaving the clinic to go into private practice. When he leaves he won't be seeing any patients for six months.

Very hot today—in the 90s—and no air-conditioning in the house.

I tried to reason with C. about not rising from bed at night, but it doesn't seem to sink in. The hard thing about this stroke so far is that physically, he's unsafe—mentally, he's unreliable. It's not a great combination. The "play the hand you're dealt" advice is hard to accept when you're in a panic.

### Thursday, July 31 – Day 44

During the night C. was up often between 2:00 and 5:00. At 6:15 he went into the living room and I followed to give him his pills and take his blood sugar. He went back to sleep in the guest room and I woke him for breakfast at 9:30. I should get him something to eat and drink earlier, and I have to watch for dehydration too. All the tasks that were being done by dozens of nursing home workers all fall to me now.

We took a drive and stopped to see some friends along the way. C. was really carrying on nice conversations today and remembering things, like the date when Judith and her kids arrive from Italy. It gave me a glimmer of hope.

### Friday, August 1 – Day 45
C. slept hardly at all. He was bouncing around on the mattress all night even when he was under my edict to stay in bed because that was the only way I knew he was safe.

Everyone at the nursing home was sympathetic when I brought him in for therapy. They said I looked wiped out. They patted me, clucked—but what to do?

I won't be able to talk to C.'s doctor or his neurologist for a while (both on vacation) or I might ask one of them for a sleeping med, even though I have reservations.

C.'s new walker arrived today, as did the floor-to-ceiling pole to put next to his bed that the physical therapist at St. Thomas had cut down to fit our bedroom. [Chuck had the pole in his room at the nursing home to assist him getting into and out of bed.] It felt good to accomplish even those little things.

### Saturday, August 2 – Day 46
I slept better and was only wakeful between 3:00 and 4:30 when he was. I may have slept through his earlier wakefulness because he said he was very tired today and took several naps. Charles and Hnoi are here, and she offered to watch Chuck while I took a walk this morning and she also made dinner. He napped all afternoon, and my nightmare is he'll wake up as soon as his head hits the pillow tonight. A woman who does home health care came over to meet us. We all thought she was a good fit, but she can't start for three weeks.

C. helped me fold laundry today. He sat on his walker and folded his hankies and some hand towels. I need to involve him more in activities like this. Tomorrow, I'll have him make his own toast!

My desire to keep writing this journal is waning. I have less time now and I question whether it's therapeutic. Others say I should keep writing because what I share in emails inspires them. I know they're trying to be kind, but the last thing I feel I can offer anyone right now is inspiration.

### Sunday, August 3 – Day 47

*Bad night. When I went into the living room at 3:00, there was evidence of his roaming—pillows and blankets on the couch—and an LP record he apparently wanted to play. He hasn't put a record on the turntable for years. He came back to bed and from 3:00 to 6:00 it seems I was cajoling him to be still, to let me sleep. I found myself getting frustrated and angry with him (inappropriate), and finally frustrated at myself for being unable to sleep. At 5:00 I got a glass of wine, quickly drank it, and that did take the edge off. Never done that before. At 6:45 he got up to get dressed, so I took his blood sugar, gave him his meds and breakfast. In the afternoon we worked on a children's world map puzzle. The only good thing about his roaming is that he seems to be moving around better. But all it takes is one stumble or loss of balance to lead to a bad fall.*

*It's been just the two of us today and he hasn't been talkative. I wonder now if there is any chance for recovery and if I will ever have the old Chuck back.*

### Monday, August 4 – Day 48

*I think I bought too enthusiastically into the idea of "reversing the effects of the stroke" concept the neurologists were peddling. I suppose many of the physical effects have been reversed—he's not paralyzed, for example, so the surgery was a success for him in that way. But tonight he couldn't remember my name, guessing first it was April, and then Sandy.*

*Took C. to the nursing home for therapy and I went to Safeway. Spent a lot of money on his new prescriptions. I am using his therapy time as respite for me, but it doesn't seem to be enough. Am feeling discouraged today. Progress ebbs and flows. There's less forward motion. Talked to our insurance agent about C.'s long-term health care policy. She has to crunch some numbers to find out whether we should apply now or wait until later. I never thought we'd need this.*

*I wondered about asking Lillie to move in with us—and would our long-term care policy pay for a live-in RN who is also a relative? The finances of all this are a big question that I'm trying not to think about right now.*

*The clinic finally returned my call to say that I need to phone the neurologist's office about a sleep medication. I called and didn't hear back from them. The occupational therapist at the nursing home suggested I take C. to Battle Point Park every day and walk him around from 4:00 to 5:00 to tire him out. I wonder if she would like to do that. Everyone has an idea, but nothing seems to work.*

**Tuesday, August 5 – Day 49**
*Another restless one. I slept in the guest room a bit. We took his walker to Fort Ward again in the morning, and he walked a ways before tiring and sitting down. A woman walked by and said, "He's lucky to have you." She couldn't have known how comforting her words were.*

*C. seemed frustrated by his word association speech therapies. He can converse, remember things, draw conclusions, but he can't see that the word "nurse" is associated with "doctor"—not "name" or "rifle." I don't get it. He did seem to get brighter at one point. Even said he had "returned."*

*By pleading with a nurse on the phone, I managed to get an appointment with C.'s neurologist in Seattle tomorrow to talk about his sleep disturbances.*

*There are still safety issues. He tries to put on and take off his pants while he's standing. I need a sturdier bath chair. Got a call from the plumber about the new grab bars and handheld showerhead. I can pick them up on Friday so I called the tile guy to see when he is available to install them and left a message. A million things to do.*

**Wednesday, August 6 – Day 50**
*C. hardly slept at all until after breakfast, then he napped from 8:00 to 10:00 a.m. when I woke him to take him to therapy. I asked a neighbor to be here for the mattress delivery and she ended up waiting for four hours! C. says the new mattress is too high.*

*We took the ferry to Seattle where Dr. Ross prescribed a sleep med, agreeing we need to get a handle on sleeping. He reminded me to schedule appointments for C. with an eye doctor and a dentist. When I asked him about C.'s cognition, he said it might improve or might not. He will take his first sleeping pill tonight and we hope for the best.*

*C. and I tried to communicate about our plans, hopes, fears in the van on the way home. I feel so alone.*

### Thursday, August 7 – Day 51

*I had to stop my last entry there because C. was insisting that he wouldn't go to sleep unless I did. In the past, it was easy for him to express his needs, and that was helpful. Now his mental state causes him to express needs that can be unreasonable. I should try to discern his real needs from his imagined needs.*

*He took his first sleeping pill. I don't know when I went to the guest room to sleep, but he fell three times around the bed last night. I helped him get back in bed each time. Then at 7:00 he fell near the toilet. When I came into the bathroom he was sitting in the middle of the floor, unable to get up. He said he was walking in his sleep. I had to get him to crawl to the bed, then kneel and use the mattress to pull himself up. He would not get in bed no matter what I said. So I did. He is very slow today. Couldn't walk at first, then was hanging out of the wheelchair sleeping—why he didn't fall out, I don't know. I had to postpone breakfast and then feed it to him.*

*I called the nursing home and talked to the admissions director and the social worker. They are prepared to take him back and it's tempting for his own safety and my sanity. I called some home health care places, and we have an appointment with one tomorrow. They'll come to the house and do an assessment and give me a rate on overnight care. I think if I could just sleep, I could do the daytime work.*

*Problem is, I have to provide a bed for the care worker and it can't be in the same room as Chuck's bed. How is that "overnight care"? How will they know if he's up and wandering around? I will have to sleep on the futon in the basement from exactly 11:00 p.m. to 6:00 a.m. because that is the company's overnight schedule.*

**Friday, August 8 – Day 52**

*I went back and forth between readmitting C. to the nursing home and opting for overnight care. I finally realized I was spent. We both talked to Isabel, handing the phone back and forth. I told her I was at the end of my tether. She told me I had to take care of myself—and that only I know how much I can take before the toll on my own physical and mental health becomes too great.*

*I fear I didn't handle the situation well, because I drove C. to the nursing home, and although we'd discussed him being readmitted, I think he thought he was only going in for therapy. When I mentioned we were going to talk to the admissions director, his face fell. Very hard morning.*

*We went to Dr. Patel who was back in his office for a few days before leaving permanently for private practice. He told C. not to view the readmission as a setback. He said he really thought C. would get better and started him on an antidepressant. Ted and I took C. back home where Ted warmed up some lunch. I made some phone calls, canceling the home assessment for night care. Maybe next week I'll set it up again.*

*I packed C. up and drove him back to the nursing home. A staff member who had been very sympathetic talked to C. and tried to get him to speak about his feelings. He told her he's depressed and angry. When I was putting up some photographs on the bulletin board in C's room, I asked him if it was all right if I used push pins. He said, "You can use nails for all I care. I'm never getting out of this place." He's back in the same double room, but fortunately he doesn't have a roommate at the moment.*

*We watched the Mariners game, then went out into the backyard and sat in the gazebo and talked and hugged. I wrote this journal entry, then went to bed and slept for eight hours straight. Made me realize what an interrupted sleep schedule I'd been having. Since I was getting some sleep I thought I was okay. I wasn't.*

### Saturday, August 9 – Day 53

*I'm experiencing a lot of negativity, anxiety, depression, and despair. Fortunately it comes and goes. There's a desperate feeling of wanting out of this life I now have, of wanting Chuck to participate more mentally in making plans for his future, of facing the progressive nature of Parkinson's and wondering if and how I can adapt the house, or if and when to transfer him to another facility, or to stay home and hire more care—how long will the money hold out, should I sell our house (so much crap to wade through)—how much do I need to give before it becomes too much? What would Chuck do with me if the tables were turned? So many thoughts, so much uncertainty.*

*Chuck in earlier days, before his stroke.*

# THE ROAD LESS TRAVELED
## 1964–1968

# 10

# It All Began
# with a Pink Wastebasket

A four-year convoluted journey led me to the moment when I became Chuck's practice teacher, and it all began with a pink wastebasket.

In the spring of 1964, my high school held an assembly to recruit juniors for a new summer school program called "Urban Studies." Everyone received an application. I brought mine home and threw it into the pink wastebasket in my bedroom because I had never attended summer school and never intended to.

The following night, I watched a program on TV that changed my mind. A news reporter interviewed student volunteers who were being trained to enroll black voters in Mississippi. For decades, Jim Crow laws had enforced segregation and made it impossible for most southern blacks to register to vote. The "Freedom Summer" volunteers aimed to change that. But they would be facing danger.

*Wow,* I thought. *I wonder if Mom and Dad would let me go. But it sounds kind of scary. Am I brave enough to do that?* Then one of the Freedom Summer trainers said words that seemed directed right at me:

"If you're coming to Mississippi, you should be prepared to be beaten, to go to jail, and maybe even be killed. If you are not, please stay home and do what you can to assist the movement from there."

*Okay.* Heaving a sigh of relief, I went upstairs and fished the Urban Studies application out of my wastebasket, filled it out, and was accepted into the program.

Every weekday that summer, along with twenty white students from my school, I rode a bus into Chicago and spent the day with twenty nonwhite students from various city high schools. In the morning we studied sociology and urban issues. Afternoons we engaged in activities like conducting apartment building inspections and planning a neighborhood street fair. On our way to these activities, we were bused through Chicago neighborhoods from Uptown to Pullman and saw low-income housing projects from Cabrini-Green to Altgeld Gardens. I never knew these places existed. That seemingly inconsequential act of removing a piece of paper from a wastebasket changed the course of my life.

Before Urban Studies, "Chicago" to me meant downtown Chicago. This included places like my grandparents' apartment on Lake Shore Drive, bustling restaurants in the Loop where I enjoyed birthday lunches with my family, the Field Museum and Adler Planetarium that I'd toured on school trips, and theaters on State Street where I'd watched epic movies like *Around the World in 80 Days* and *Oklahoma!*

After my Urban Studies experience, "Chicago" also meant segregated neighborhoods, poverty, and gun violence. It meant rival gangs fighting for turf, political dissembling, and schools in shameful need of repair.

I was not brave enough to become a Freedom Summer volunteer, but that was okay. My summer school experience forged my commitment to address urban problems in whatever ways I could.

During my senior year of high school, I volunteered on Saturdays at a day-care center in one of Chicago's Polish neighborhoods, an activity I never would have pursued had it not been for the Urban Studies program.

And after my freshman year of college, in the summer of 1966 (when "Hot Town, Summer in the City" blared over radios), I drove to the University of Chicago twice a week to tutor Pam, an African American high school graduate who wanted extra studies to prepare for college. Pam and I sat on a park bench on the South Side's Midway Plaisance studying Chaucer, Tennessee Williams, *King Lear*, and grammar—all those subjects I thought were essential to an advanced education. I also helped her fill out college applications.

After our sessions I would drop her off at her apartment, which was located over a storefront grocery with peeling green paint. The first time I saw her home, my heart filled with sadness. But gradually, I realized that Pam's dream to be the first in her family to earn a college degree was not only an exit strategy from her blighted neighborhood, it also meant that her commitment to education was greater than mine. I rarely even thought about the fact that my grandmother paid my tuition at a private liberal arts college.

At the end of August, the Central YMCA Community College in the Loop mailed Pam an acceptance letter! We celebrated with cupcakes on the Midway. We had one more session scheduled the following week, but Pam called to cancel it. When I asked why, she told me that her fifteen-year-old nephew had been shot and killed when he refused to join a gang. She mourned her nephew, but Pam was proud of her brother because he'd agreed to do the unthinkable: testify against his son's killers, only boys themselves.

I never learned what happened after that, and I assumed I'd never see Pam again.

But the following summer, she mailed me an invitation to her wedding. I parked outside the small church on the South Side where Pam and Thomas, a Chicago policeman, would be married. I had not been in "the ghetto" in several months, and suddenly I felt afraid. I walked nervously to the front door of the church where I was greeted by Pam's parents. "You must be Florrie! Welcome!"

"Yes," I said, returning their hugs. I wondered how they knew who I was, until I looked around and saw elegantly dressed African Americans in every pew. One woman scooted over and gestured for me to sit next to her. Pam was delighted that I'd made it to their wedding, and I felt ashamed of my racist reaction to revisiting her neighborhood.

As I finished my junior year of college, I realized I needed to make a career decision. Though it was the late '60s and a time of great change and liberalism, it seemed to me I had only three job choices: nurse, secretary, or teacher. I knew I was no nurse, and I hadn't gone to college to learn how to be a secretary. That left teaching, which meant I needed to take some education courses and complete a semester of practice teaching.

My next choice was where to teach. I could stay in Wisconsin and teach in Oshkosh, Neenah-Menasha, or some other small town. Or I could join a new "Urban Studies Practice Teaching Program" offered by the Associated Colleges of the Midwest, an organization representing ten liberal arts schools. Program participants would live in an old residential hotel in Hyde Park, an integrated neighborhood not far from the Midway Plaisance, and each practice teacher would undertake two assignments in two different socioeconomic neighborhoods. Maybe it was the familiar sound of "Urban Studies Program," or perhaps it was the edginess and risk-taking that characterized that era and my age. But I felt emboldened by the example of my sister Carol's life, so my decision was to take the road less traveled—and to practice teach in Chicago.

Prior to my move to Hyde Park, I spent a week at a resort near Jackson Hole, Wyoming, with my parents and two aunts. The week was filled with horseback rides, boat trips on the Snake River, and elegant meals served by Mexican waiters. It was no preparation for what was to come.

The night we flew home from Wyoming—August 28, 1968—I stood curbside at O'Hare Airport with a transistor radio pressed to my ear listening to news reports coming from the Democratic National Convention in downtown Chicago. Ten thousand demonstrators had gathered that day in Grant Park for a legal rally that included speeches and songs. Unbeknownst to me, one of those present was a high school teacher named Chuck Munat who had heard the media reports and wanted to be an eyewitness to what happened. In midafternoon, police advanced into the park and began beating demonstrators with batons. Journalists with cameras were singled out. Some people returned the abuse, throwing rocks and chunks of cement, and the peaceful affair deteriorated into what the Walker Report would later term "a police riot." Chuck and hundreds of other onlookers became trapped in the park and were not allowed to emerge until several hours later after dark.

Just about the time I was tuning in my radio, Chuck was being pushed and shoved down Michigan Avenue and maced by a Chicago police officer while TV cameras rolled and the crowd chanted, "The whole world is watching! The whole world is watching!" Police and National Guardsmen continued to use clubs and tear gas on protesters outside the Hilton, causing fumes to drift into the hotel, including the room of Democratic presidential candidate Hubert Humphrey.

A medic washed Chuck's burning eyes with water from a canteen, and he returned home. He later said he had become radicalized that night.

Fifteen miles north of the rioting, my parents and I arrived back at our house. I listened to the radio long into the night, as more drama unfolded inside the convention at the Chicago Amphitheatre. Announcers reported that during his presidential nominating speech of George McGovern, Connecticut Senator Abraham Ribicoff had described the police actions on the streets of Chicago as "Gestapo tactics," and Mayor Richard J. Daley had yelled profanities at Ribicoff.

I lay in my bed reflecting on how John F. Kennedy's Camelot continued to unravel, with the assassinations of Martin Luther King Jr. and Bobby Kennedy earlier in the year, and now this violent clash between police and demonstrators that victimized and traumatized so many citizens—while politicians did little except bully one another.

It seemed an inauspicious time to enter that tinderbox as a practice teacher, but three days later I moved into the Del Prado Hotel in Hyde Park. And because of some complicated tangle of random events and choices that began with my taking a summer school application out of a pink wastebasket, my life and the life of Chuck Munat, inner-city high school teacher, were about to intersect.

# 11

# Peace and Love

Metal tables and chairs had been configured into rows in the high school gym. As faculty and administrators entered and greeted one another after the long summer recess, the gym got louder by the minute. I had been one of the first to arrive for this meeting. I quickly found a table designated by a small sign: "Mr. Munat – Chairman, English Dept." and sat down.

I had no clue how to pronounce his name, nor did I have any idea of his age or what he looked like. I kept watching the door as teacher after teacher entered and voices reverberated against the gym's yellow brick walls. *Is that him? Nope. Is that him?*

Shortly before 9:00 a.m., I saw a thirty-something man with thick gray hair and a beard (but no mustache) standing in the doorway. He wore black pants and a white short-sleeved shirt, its pocket crammed with pencils, and as he gazed around the gym he looked slightly amused. I knew right away he had to be Mr. Munat.

He made his way across the gym, saying hello to a few fellow teachers, and approached the Mr. Munat table where I introduced myself as his new practice teacher. He smiled and said, "You mean I got one?" He looked welcoming and pleased—whether that was because he was a friendly guy or because he'd just learned that his teaching load had been reduced, I couldn't tell. But he made me feel comfortable right away. When I asked how to pronounce his name, he replied, "muh-NAHT, as in monotonous."

He told me he'd had a practice teacher the year before, so he hadn't expected another one but was happy to have me. He explained that he taught five sophomore classes—three "Regular" English and two "College" English (using the Chicago Public School track system terms). I would observe all his classes for two weeks, and then pick two that I wanted to teach for the next six weeks, after which I would move on to my second school.

I observed a lot during the first few days of classes. When students poured into the mobile unit at the start of a period, Mr. Munat would be sitting at his desk doing paperwork. The bell would ring, but the students kept chattering. Mr. Munat would continue working. I'd wait for him to bring the class to order by yelling or telling them to settle down. He didn't. Eventually they quieted down on their own and turned their attention to him, at which point he would look up from his papers and say, "Ready?"

He loved his students, especially his "Regular" students, ninety-five percent of whom were African Americans. He told them he knew that when they were outside the classroom they spoke a dialectical street language—and he found that kind of speech not only acceptable but also beautifully creative. He called their dialect "Care*free* American" and created writing projects in which he collected some of their expressions, especially their "sigs." The art of "signifying" is a Chicago form of recreation, a word game in which one person tries to out-insult the other. Insults often involve economic or physical inadequacies—and often target the other player's mother, such as:

"Your mama so low she play handball off the curb."

"Your mama live so far in the earth, they got to pump in daylight to her."

"Your mama so old she exhale dust."

"Your mama so black she leave footprints in a coal mine."

At an English department meeting that fall, Mr. Munat showed his colleagues a compilation of his students' signifying, which he had divided into categories. A young black teacher complained, "What is this all about? What does this mean: 'Your mama so dirty she leave a bath ring 'round Lake Michigan'?"

Mr. Munat answered, "Miss Green, that is hyperbole Shakespeare would have been proud of."

On the other hand, Mr. Munat told his students he expected them to learn what he called "Care*ful* American" for more formal occasions, like in the classroom or at job interviews. I tried to follow his lead when I taught his first- and second-period Regular English classes, but I knew I fell way short of his standard. Mr. Munat was supportive of me, but left me alone in the mobile unit so they would truly be my students. When my six weeks was up, I moved on to my second assignment in the South Shore neighborhood.

*In 1977, Chuck took a leave from his writing job to teach at Connecticut's only juvenile correctional facility. He began a school newspaper and said, "Kids who could not write are writing* The Nameless News, *and kids who could not read are reading it."*

In late October, Mr. Munat moved to a one-room apartment a few blocks away from his family, and a few blocks from the Del Prado Hotel. And somewhere around that time, he and I fell in love. I would like to tell you exactly when and how that happened. Clearly, I admired his actions on the day of the student demonstration and in the classroom, and maybe he admired me for making the journey from the suburbs to the inner city. But admiration doesn't translate into the kind of love we experienced. I can only say that we needed each other to be at peace.

Only our closest friends knew about our relationship. So we needed to find a spot where we could meet privately after school, and Chuck knew just the place.

A few blocks from the high school stood a stone building that housed one of Hyde Park's synagogues. Etched in stone, high above its wooden doors, were the words: "My Hovse Is a Hovse of Worship for All People." That temple became our rendezvous.

From there it was a short walk to the pedestrian tunnel that passed underneath Lake Shore Drive and out onto the 57th Street Beach, transporting us to our place of peace. He carried a US Army satchel from his post-college military days, and he gave me a faded striped pillowcase to sling over my shoulder as a collection bag. As cars sped by during rush hour, Chuck and I would walk the beach, heads down, poking piles of seaweed with long sticks as we searched for our special treasures.

What were we looking for? Little bits of driftwood mostly. Pieces of wood whose beauty, as Chuck explained to me, had been shaped by the four elements: water, air, earth/sand, and sometimes fire. He said that unlike the ocean, Lake Michigan is gentle with its driftwood.

Over the years Chuck had found many intriguing pieces, which he took into his home workshop to varnish. Applying the first coat of varnish was the most exciting part of the process because he never knew exactly how a piece of wood would turn out. Something plain-looking might reveal magnificent lines or colors. Something you thought beautiful might turn out to be dull. It was the duty of the artist, he said, to let the wood determine what it should become. An artist could destroy a piece by imposing his own sense of beauty. He gave me many of his best creations, each with a tiny hook at the top so I could wear them on a chain around my neck.

We didn't limit our collection to driftwood only. We picked up other things that caught our attention: a special shell, a colorful piece of lake glass, a bit of rusted tin, a pale-orange crayfish claw.

After school we usually spent about an hour on the beach. Then when only the last few rays of sun were visible behind the museum dome across Lake Shore Drive, we would walk back through the underpass and say, "Peace and love," to one another in front of the Hovse of Worship.

Having spent my childhood summers in the Rocky Mountains, I thought something had to be thirteen thousand feet tall to be beautiful. Chuck taught me that beauty is everywhere—even in a pile of seaweed. This was one of the many lessons I would learn from him.

*After school Chuck and I walked*
*the 57th Street Beach searching for driftwood.*

# *SHATTERED*
## *August–October 2003*

# Hitting Rock Bottom

Chuck's readmission to St. Thomas Health & Rehabilitation Center was followed by a period of extreme anxiety and uncertainty for me. The plan was still to bring him home; we were just waiting for improvement in his balance, cognition, and safety awareness.

Instead, he moved backward in all of these areas.

Alone in his room, Chuck fell or lurched against the walls. When a therapist noticed his regression in balance, she suggested he wear a helmet to protect himself from head injuries, and he agreed. Because he wasn't showing improvement, therapists told me it would be difficult to convince Medicare to continue paying for his therapy—and therefore, his stay at St. Thomas. I translated this to mean that I would have to bring him home in worse condition than he was the first time. Either that, or private pay, which I didn't think we could afford.

When discharge dates were set, my anxiety about home care rose. But when those dates were rescinded because of Chuck's confusion or ability to self-care, my hopes for a return to normal life were shattered.

I spoke with an administrator who implied that St. Thomas couldn't keep Chuck there against his will. If he wanted to come home, they couldn't stop him. This thought threw me into a panic. I stunned myself by imagining the possibility of divorcing him. I could give him our house and half our estate so he'd have a place to live and money for home health care, and I would live somewhere else. I never seriously considered this option, but the fact that I even imagined it shows how terrified I was.

Ted offered to travel to our house and spend three nights a week as Chuck's overnight caregiver. But that plan fell through when he got a new job in Olympia.

Doctors, nurses, therapists, and aides proposed a variety of reasons for Chuck's regression. Some thought he'd had another stroke or a series of TIAs. Others said that he could be having adverse reactions to his medications for Parkinson's and depression. Or he could still be experiencing the aftereffects of his first stroke and/or the anesthetic administered during tPA. A therapist told me that dehydration could be the culprit.

Or could it be something else—something we hadn't yet considered?

The nursing home therapists didn't give up. They worked hard with Chuck, and he did everything they asked. But it became obvious that he was inexplicably losing ground and that it would be unsafe for him to come home until he'd showed some improvement. When yet another discharge date was postponed because he hadn't reached his inpatient therapy goals, Chuck sobbed, "I'm devastated!"

All I could do was hold him.

*Chuck with his sister Judith and brother Stan.*

Not long after his readmission, Chuck's sister Judith and her two adult children arrived from their home in Florence, Italy. I enjoyed their company and that of our family who came to visit their Italian relatives. But most nights when I came home from St. Thomas, I was so worn out from overseeing Chuck's care that facing a houseful of people felt overwhelming.

One night Judith, bless her, cooked a Mexican meal for eight. In the middle of dinner preparations, I heard cries from the kitchen. "Florrie! The sink is leaking!"

Cilantro leaves floated in a gray lake that was spreading across the kitchen floor. I called a plumber who made a night call ($$$), after which I ate a burrito, tried to be sociable, then retreated to our bedroom and wrote in my journal: "Sometimes I don't know how I hold back the demons." The following night, the sink leaked again.

When I wasn't with Chuck, I worried about him. So I spent most of my waking hours at the nursing home because I felt less anxious when we were together. My knee-jerk response to our disaster was to dedicate my full attention to Chuck: sitting with him in his room, observing his therapy sessions, telephoning doctors and insurance agents, filling prescriptions, and watching him sleep. At home, I faced the chores of lawn-mowing, watering our new flower beds, doing laundry (previously Chuck's domain), hauling garbage and recycling to the curb, cleaning house, paying bills, etc. I felt as if I'd jumped into a giant sinkhole and we were both drowning.

Even if I had recognized that my efforts far exceeded what was reasonable or even good for us, I don't think I could have pulled in my caregiving reins and slowed that runaway wagon. I felt compelled to heave all my energies into this catastrophe until I'd fixed it. I would be Super Caregiver! In hindsight, it was self-centered magical thinking to assume that I could control Chuck's illness. But I couldn't seem to grasp that I had launched myself on a solo mission that was doomed.

Others could see it.

At a family and staff Care Conference at St. Thomas, our son Charles shared that he and his siblings were worried that I was on the verge of a breakdown. Sharon, the director of nursing, followed up his remark by saying, "Chuck, your wife is going to take a little rest. She won't be spending as much time with you from now on."

Though I was surprised that Sharon had made the decision for us, I sensed she was right. I had learned to rely on her judgment and to seek her opinions on caregiving matters. I also learned that when her explosive temperament surfaced—you could tell by the angry flashes in her eyes—it was better to wait before approaching her. But Sharon had a wealth of geriatric experience. Most importantly, her decisions were motivated by compassion for the residents and supporting her staff.

After the conference, Sharon took me aside and addressed me alone. "If you don't slow down, *you* could die first." Her words gave me pause. But if I stayed away from the nursing home, I would feel like I had abandoned Chuck. I couldn't do that.

I was experiencing a frightening upsurge of emotions: anxiety, confusion, fear, sadness, guilt, despair, remorse, and outrage at the circumstances that were tearing our previous life to shreds. I could not bury those emotions. And the only way to be calm while I lived through them was to spend most of my waking moments with Chuck. So despite all the good reasons to follow Sharon's advice, I largely ignored it.

Though I was sleeping better than I had during Chuck's home stay, I continued to toss and turn in our bed. I felt relieved that he was somewhere safer, but I missed his presence. I awoke often in the night, scared to be alone in our big house and worried about having to fill the sole caregiver role again. Some mornings I didn't want to get out of bed. When a rash broke out on my arms, legs, and shoulders, my doctor prescribed an anti-itch cream, and she also gave me a mild sleeping pill. She told me that I needed to take care of myself if I expected to be healthy enough to function as Chuck's caregiver.

One August afternoon, Chuck and I were sitting in the backyard gazebo at St. Thomas. Tall Douglas firs surrounded us, blocking the sunlight. Deb, the head of therapy, had just cancelled Chuck's discharge date—again—due to his inability to walk and transfer safely. She guessed that it might take months to correct his balance. A chickadee broke the silence. Long ago, Chuck had taught me to remember its song by the phrase "Drink Your Tea," but today he didn't notice the birdsong. He turned slightly in his wheelchair to face me.

He said, "I'm very disappointed in you for keeping me here. We didn't really try things at home."

Feeling like he'd just plunged a knife into my chest, I wanted to get up and leave. *Let him figure out how to get back to his room. I don't care!* After everything I'd sacrificed, he wanted more. But I had no more to give; I was a dry well.

We sat in silence, both of us angry and sad. Two months ago in the emergency room, I'd agreed to the tPA procedure, believing that Chuck would make a full recovery. Now I gazed at the shell of the man who had made me laugh, given me strength to believe in our love when everyone else was opposed, and taught me innumerable lessons about life—such as to be brave and not give up hope.

Looking thoughtful, Chuck said, "What's going to happen will happen." His words were more philosophic than any I could have mustered at that moment.

I rose and pushed his wheelchair back to his room and got him settled for the night. I knew that committing Chuck to this nursing home had been the right decision. He knew it had been the wrong decision. We so rarely disagreed about anything. The fact that we disagreed now on a matter of such consequence shot waves of despair through my body. I hoped we'd hit rock bottom. Because if things got any worse, I didn't know what I would do.

# 13

# Everything Florrie Does for Me

I had to find a new doctor for Chuck. Dr. Patel had now left our local clinic to establish an off-island practice that wouldn't open for six months. With Chuck in desperate need of immediate and excellent care, I decided to return to Dr. Farmer, who'd been our physician when we moved to the island fourteen years ago. I transferred Chuck's medical records to him, and he immediately began to study Chuck's case. His nurse scheduled another CAT scan for Chuck, as well as appointments at Seattle's Bennett Hospital with Dr. Ross the neurologist and Dr. Chan, head of rehab. And she gave me Dr. Farmer's cell phone number, which I could call 24/7. Having him on board was a huge relief to me, and Chuck was happy to have his former doctor back.

A few weeks later Dr. Farmer, a tall, blond man with wire-rimmed glasses, stood at St. Thomas's nursing station reading through the pages of Chuck's medical chart. When I approached the desk, he looked up.

"What do you think about Chuck coming home to live?" I asked. I was still seeking assurance that readmitting him had been the right decision.

He closed the chart book and looked at me. "How much do you feel like Superwoman?" I shrugged.

He said, "Look, anyone can live at home if you create a hospital setting. But I think you'd be nuts to do that."

"But ... do you think he's going to get better?"

His blue eyes softened. "Let's just say he's not coming home anytime soon. He needs twenty-four-hour care right now."

Never did I want Chuck to have to live in a nursing home. But neither could I imagine caring for him at home with his current needs. This was yet another conversation that made me both enormously relieved and extraordinarily sad. As time passed and Chuck did not get better, I realized that I needed to create a new life—but I resisted that notion like the flu. I was addicted to being his caregiver, and that's all I wanted to be.

I received tremendous help in my recovery when I started seeing a therapist. After an Eldercare Conference at St. Thomas, I picked up a business card someone had left behind that offered geriatric case management from a woman named Sue. When I phoned her, she said that Chuck's case management was a possibility for later, but in the meantime would I like to see her for a few private sessions?

Sue's counseling became my lifeline during Chuck's early months at St. Thomas. I told her the story of our turned-upside-down life, and she listened and reinforced my role as Chuck's caregiver while simultaneously encouraging me to pursue a life of my own—and she insisted that I deserved one. Seeing a therapist was one of my first admissions that I could not do this Herculean caregiving job without help.

During my late-afternoon therapy sessions in a house two blocks from St. Thomas, I would begin to cry and then choke back my tears.

"Don't do that," Sue would say, pushing a box of tissues across her desk. "Let it go. Crying gets the hurt out of you."

"But I don't want to cry," I would sniffle.

"Why?"

"Because if I'm crying, I can't talk!"

"Yes. But why else?"

"Because ... if I start crying, I don't think I'll be able to stop."

Sue gently led me to the understanding that the task I had undertaken—the restoration of our previous life—was impossible. And I'd been feeling crippling guilt over my inability to do it! If I were going to survive, she said, I needed to carve out a new life separate from my old life with Chuck. At first, I didn't realize I needed to do that for my own emotional and spiritual health, so I continued to devote myself slavishly to Chuck's care.

Sue counseled me, "The fact that you needed to put your husband in a nursing home doesn't mean you're not competent, doesn't mean you're not lovable, doesn't mean you don't care, doesn't mean you don't love him."

I was shocked that I'd been harboring those very assumptions, though I couldn't have articulated them until she did it for me. I had convinced myself that I should be able to do everything and was failing miserably—when in fact, I was doing all I could.

Sue helped me understand that people are in nursing homes not because they are unloved, but because caregivers have limits. And I finally realized that what Chuck wanted was not necessarily "to come home," which would have been just a larger version of the nursing home. He wanted his former life back—and that I could not do.

One day I told Chuck I was going home to write another email update about him to our friends and family. He said, without emotion, "Tell them I feel alone and forgotten." After his readmission, the resident care coordinator had talked with Chuck about his depression. Chuck told her, "No one ever asks me how I'm feeling." Those statements were not self-pitying; they were facts. Chuck had always been a realist.

But in my guilty, grieving condition, I could not bring myself to ask him, "How are you feeling?" I was afraid his answers would reveal my failings. I'm grateful to Chuck's sister Judith, who asked him the questions I was too scared to ask.

While sitting with him at St. Thomas one day, Judith said, "What is the worst thing about your life now?"

"Being institutionalized," Chuck told her.

"But you understand why you have to be here."

"Oh, yes. Florrie could never take care of me at home."

"And what is the best thing about your life now?"

"Everything that Florrie does for me."

# 14

# My Behavior This Morning
# Was Exemplary

In September, Chuck began to experience delusions and hallucinations, which added another layer of confusion to his diagnosis. What was wrong with him? His new behavior shocked me. One night he telephoned 9-1-1 and reported that he had not made any arrests. After he hung up, the dispatcher called St. Thomas to make sure that Charles Munat was a resident. The next morning when the hall nurse told me about this, she was laughing. Maybe his phone call was funny to her, but not to me.

Another time Deb, the head of therapy, reported that Chuck had carried his dresser drawer down the hall, warning the nurses: "A fire is going to engulf the building. Everyone must find a place of safety." He said he had read about the fire in a book, and added, "It's going to be a very sad day."

Chuck didn't remember these episodes afterward. So when Deb asked Chuck to sign a form permitting the therapy department to videotape him when he was having such an experience, Chuck agreed. When lucid, he seemed curious about his own behavior.

Chuck became particularly confused in the early mornings when he would rise and act out "dreams," as he called his hallucinations. One morning a grim-faced nurse told me that at 5:30 a.m., Chuck had disarmed the front security door (by punching in the 1-2-3-4 code which was posted on the keypad) and tried to leave the building. When an aide stood in the door blocking him, my dear pacifist husband punched her five times in the chest.

At a Care Conference that afternoon, Chuck explained that he'd been trying to rescue two people by taking them outside. One of them was a badly wounded man whom Chuck was carrying on his back. Maybe the man Chuck was trying to save was himself.

One night a nurse found him crouching beside his bed, insisting he was in a foxhole and people were shooting at him. Then Hitler came to visit, driving a car he called Stallion; it was at the end of the war, and the Führer needed money. Next came Mrs. Stonehausen (who was actually Mrs. Hitler) and her three dead children. Chuck told me that men, women, and children came down a stairway next to his bed every night to sleep in the room beneath his. The nursing home had no stairs and no basement.

September 8 was the day that Dr. Farmer's nurse had scheduled back-to-back appointments with Dr. Ross and Dr. Chan in Seattle. That morning Chuck rose, dressed, and left the facility at 5:45 a.m. When an aide tried to stop him from leaving, Chuck banged his walker on the ground and shouted at her, and she'd been unable to redirect him. This aide wisely decided not to stand in his way. Instead, she and an RN followed him for half a mile as he raced down the sidewalk with his walker. At least he was observing proper safety precautions! When he reached a major intersection, he turned his walker around, sat down on the seat, and told the women, "My wife will be picking me up here."

When my phone rang at 5:50 a.m., I heard a nurse say that my husband had just disarmed the nursing home's security door again and was walking into town. I groggily asked if she could bring him the phone so I could talk to him.

"Oh, no," she said, "he's much too far away." As I pondered that statement, she asked, "Do you want to come get him or shall we call the police?"

*Those are my options?*

"I'll come get him."

I threw on some clothes and sped into town. As I drove down the empty main street I spied Chuck, wearing his red plaid jacket and wide-brimmed leather hat, sitting on his walker while two women in scrubs stood nearby smoking. I had no trouble finding a parking place.

I approached him. "Chuck, what are you doing?"

"I fought hard for you," he answered. Wondering if that was a quote from *Romeo and Juliet*, I transferred a now-amenable Chuck into the van and drove him back up the street. I offered the women in scrubs a ride, but they said they'd walk. I put Chuck in bed and he immediately fell asleep.

I tried to sleep in my car, but once again my husband's bizarre behavior had left me distraught. An hour later, I loaded him back into the van and drove to the ferry, which arrived late in Seattle. So I raced up to the hospital, but Dr. Ross was behind schedule so we spent thirty minutes waiting for our appointment. As planned, our son Charles joined us. While Chuck dozed, Charles shared information about graduate schools he was considering. Though I was too distracted to listen, I was grateful for his presence because unlike me, he was clear-headed and could retain information.

When we were summoned into Dr. Ross's office, he looked as charming and hopeful as always, but said, "I hear our guy's not doing so well."

I attempted to reduce the events of the past several weeks into three sentences. I mentioned that Chuck was now off the antidepressant that Dr. Patel had prescribed, which may have improved his cognition a little bit. I added, "Dr. Farmer said you've seen Chuck's CAT scan and can tell us what it showed."

Leafing through Chuck's file, Dr. Ross said, "I didn't know he'd had a CAT scan. It's not in here. Let me check the computer." I was wondering if this crazy trip had all been for nothing when he said, "Oh, here are the CAT scan results, and this is good: he didn't have a second stroke, and the original stroke site has resolved. His stroke recovery is actually going very well."

"Going well?" said Charles. His dark brown hair was prematurely turning gray just like his father's had. He glanced meaningfully at Chuck whose focus appeared to be on the skyscrapers outside the window instead of the conversation concerning his future.

"Mr. Munat's left-side brain hemisphere was occluded during the stroke. If it weren't for the tPA procedure, he would be paralyzed. *If* he survived. So yes, his stroke recovery is going well."

"But everyone agrees he's regressing," I said. "Do you have any ideas why?"

Dr. Ross said, "That's hard to say." Charles and I traded grimaces, anticipating more runaround. Chuck continued to stare out the window.

Dr. Ross continued, "But we can rule some things out now. He's been on the Parkinson's med for two months, so his Parkinson's symptoms should have improved. But I watched him shuffle in here on his walker. His face still shows very little expression. He's non-blinking, his voice is soft, and he's drooling. So it's doubtful that he has Parkinson's."

That Chuck had not had another stroke and did not have Parkinson's disease seemed to be good news. But Dr. Ross didn't look like he was getting ready to uncork the champagne.

"Well, what *does* he have then?" asked Charles.

"I don't know," Dr. Ross admitted. "Certain Parkinson-related conditions are possibilities. I'm going to give you some brochures on those to look over at home. And I want to schedule Mr. Munat to see Dr. Navarro, who's our expert on those conditions. He'll be able to give you a clearer picture. In the meantime, I'm going to reduce his Parkinson's med by one-quarter because it can cause nighttime confusion. Dr. Navarro can decide if he wants to stop it altogether."

Before I could absorb all this new information, we were whisked off to our appointment with Dr. Chan. Her main message was that Chuck should continue his three therapies (physical, occupational, speech), and she told me I'd made the right decision to place him in the skilled nursing facility. The remainder of the appointment had something to do with the timing of Medicare payments. I spaced out, which Dr. Chan must have sensed because she addressed her comments to Charles. It was midafternoon by the time we left Bennett Hospital, and Charles headed back to work in the University District.

When the ferry docked on the island, I was eager to get Chuck settled back at St. Thomas so I could go home and pour myself a stiff drink. It had been a long day, and I was feeling pretty sorry for myself. As we neared the nursing home, I couldn't resist a little nag. "I wasn't happy with your behavior this morning, you know."

Chuck drew himself up tall in the passenger seat and declared, "I thought my behavior this morning was exemplary."

I had to laugh. Say what you will about this former English teacher's sense of reality. He still had a pretty fine vocabulary.

Here are some of Chuck's word substitutions caused by aphasia (loss of ability to express or understand speech because of brain damage):

| *Intended Word* | *Chuck's Substitution* |
|---|---|
| Kaliber (nonalcoholic beer) | foreign beverage |
| certified nursing aide (CNA) | nun |
| diaper | waffle |
| whirlpool bath | the hurricane, H.O., rubbity-dubbity |
| coffee shop | cowboy shop |
| Seattle | Atlanta, Los Angeles, Chicago |
| Q-Tip | matchstick |
| wheelchair | trike |
| electric wheelchair | moped |
| walker | chariot |
| Curves (women's gym) | ovaries |
| push me | tip me over |
| cell phone | radio |
| Mariners (Seattle's baseball team) | White Sox (Chicago's baseball team) |
| cup | cat |
| emails | e.m.'s, m.e.'s |
| prunes | food you eat in Oklahoma |
| Seahawks (Seattle's football team) | Catwalks |
| runny nose | solutions from nose |
| computer | cadaver |
| chocolate pudding | black soda |
| sleepwalking | jaywalking |
| nursing home | funeral home |

15

## We Will Take Care of Him

Three days later, I drove Chuck back to Bennett Hospital for an appointment with Dr. Navarro, the Parkinson's specialist. The Doogie Howser doctor image has become a stereotype, but I swear Dr. Navarro looked like he was seventeen years old, with light-brown hair and cheeks that had never known a razor. He gave Chuck several neurological tests and came to the same conclusion as Dr. Ross: Chuck did *not* have Parkinson's disease. He based his conclusion primarily on the absence of tremor and the fact that the Parkinson's medication had not affected Chuck's Parkinson-like symptoms.

More importantly, he theorized that Chuck had a "Parkinson-Plus syndrome," and described two possible mimickers. The first was multiple system atrophy (MSA). The second was Lewy body dementia (LBD).

Back at home I reread the brochure Dr. Ross had given me on Lewy body dementia and did some online research. The central feature of LBD is dementia, defined as "a progressive cognitive decline." What I read next both horrified and enlightened me. Horrified, because I never thought Chuck might have dementia; we assumed his cognitive problems were all stroke-related. Enlightened, because the characteristics of Lewy body dementia read like a catalog of Chuck's symptoms over the past four months—and when I thought about it, even earlier.

- Fluctuating cognition
- Disorganized speech and conversation
- Hallucinations and delusions
- Parkinsonism
- Severe sensitivity to certain medications
- Repeated falls

- Anger, sadness, depression
- Difficulty swallowing, choking
- Balance difficulties
- Sleep disturbances, insomnia
- Reduced attention span, staring into space
- Abnormal result on SPECT or PET scans

On October 9, Chuck and I returned to Bennett Hospital for a SPECT scan, to be followed by a second appointment with young Dr. Navarro. Thankfully, this time Chuck waited at St. Thomas for me to pick him up, and we reported to the hospital radiology department at 10:00.

Though he hadn't slept all night, Chuck wanted to take the test alone. He wobbled into the examining room on his walker. An hour later he reappeared, complaining that the test had been horrible. He'd been put on a metal table and instructed by a technician to lie still, but he was so uncomfortable he'd squirmed continuously while a machine hovered over his head. I regretted allowing him to take the test by himself and resigned myself to returning for another scan.

We ate lunch in the hospital cafeteria (nauseatingly familiar after many meals eaten there during Chuck's three-week stay at Bennett) and rode the elevator upstairs to meet Charles, Hnoi, and Isabel at Dr. Navarro's office. Chuck stayed in his wheelchair while the rest of us found chairs in the large examining room.

Dr. Navarro entered, and the first words out of his mouth were, "The scan showed areas of brain deterioration consistent with Lewy body dementia."

Tears sprang to my eyes. I'd expected it, but somehow I hadn't expected it. We all sat in silence until Chuck asked, "Is there any other..."

"Only Alzheimer's."

"If I'd heard you say that a few months ago," Chuck said, "I wouldn't have wanted to go on living." He didn't elaborate.

"He was moving around during the scan," I said. "Could that have affected the results?"

Dr. Navarro shook his head and leaned against the examining table.

"Here's what I think has happened. Physical decline and memory loss from Lewy body dementia usually occur slowly. But when a person with LBD experiences a major brain insult—like a stroke—that can speed things up." He looked at Chuck who was staring at him. "You've probably had Lewy body dementia for months, maybe even years. If you hadn't had the stroke, you'd still be living at home, not using a walker, but dealing with gradual loss of brain function and mobility. You would eventually have arrived where you are today, just not as fast."

We asked a few halfhearted questions, one about the dangers of the disease.

"Dementia per se isn't fatal," he said. "But a person with Lewy body typically ends up suffering debilitations brought on by pneumonia, bedsores, urinary or kidney infections, broken hips, or lack of exercise that leads to being bedridden." He looked around the room. "Is there anything else you'd like to ask?"

We sat in silence. What was there to say? Everything. And nothing. Because now we knew our lives had not merely been altered. Our lives had been shattered. No longer was the future a road trailing dimly into the woods. Our road had been firebombed, and we were now peering into a black chasm.

Dr. Navarro added, "I anticipated this diagnosis based on my observations and your descriptions of his behavior, but I wanted to wait for the SPECT scan results to be sure. As sure as I can be."

I knew what he was leaving unsaid. The brochure stated that LBD, like most dementias, can only be definitively diagnosed by postmortem brain autopsy.

Chuck and I were quiet on the way home. We didn't talk, except when he expressed a desire for ice cream, so I bought him an ice cream sandwich on the ferry. Back at St. Thomas, I combed the chocolate crumbs from his beard and turned on the Red Sox–Yankees playoff game. He didn't care about those teams, but it was the best I could do. And then I said good night and wished him a good sleep.

Out in the hallway I saw Sharon, and when I told her about Chuck's diagnosis, I wept. She hugged me and said, "We will take care of him." They were the kindest words I'd heard all day.

# *STRUGGLING TO ADAPT*

## *October–December 2003*

# My Caregiving Marathon

We had a new diagnosis: a disease with the cartoonish name of Lewy body dementia. Only Sharon and a few others on the nursing home staff had some familiarity with this type of dementia. None of our family and friends had ever heard of it. Chuck could have recovered from a stroke, but not from dementia.

Chuck had a new permanent residence: St. Thomas Health & Rehabilitation Center, a skilled nursing facility five miles from the dream home we'd bought fourteen years earlier. He would not live in that house again.

A new chapter lay ahead: the rest of our life together. Dementia was not fatal, so how long would this chapter last? No one could tell us. Four months after Chuck's stroke, my caregiving sprint ended and my caregiving marathon began.

After Chuck's diagnosis and what it meant for our future, I finally accepted that I needed to stop spending my entire day with him. After some experimenting, I settled on a schedule of seeing him in the afternoons. He and I had always practiced punctuality. When we went to a movie, we were often the first to arrive at the empty theater, which gave rise to Chuck's perennial joke: "All the good seats are taken." Given our habit of being on time, plus Chuck's dependence on my daily presence, I chose to arrive at 2:00 and leave when dinner was served at 5:30. Three and a half hours would give me ample time to help with his personal hygiene (bathing, dressing, toothbrushing) and allow us to take outings—like drives around the island and bakery visits.

We valued our afternoons outside the nursing home. They gave us time away from Chuck's room and his current roommate. I felt that any opportunity for Chuck to be out in the "real world" was good for him in every way, even if that only meant that he could observe people riding bicycles or walking on the sidewalks as we drove by.

When Chuck asked if he could come back to our house for the afternoon, I balked for a couple of reasons. There were the practicalities: the time involved in driving home and back, and the difficulty of getting him and his walker or wheelchair up the front steps. But the main reason I didn't want to bring him home was that whenever he entered the house, it reminded me that we no longer lived there together. And if we couldn't return to our old life, I wanted none of it.

*Chuck, Ted, and I out for a drive shortly after Chuck's LBD diagnosis.*

Instead, we settled on an alternative plan for the afternoons that worked for both of us. In retirement we had established the habit of my reading aloud to Chuck. This started in 1989 during our summer road trip when we moved from Connecticut to Washington. That trip was possibly the longest cross-country drive in American history because Chuck insisted on visiting every friend and relative along the way. He also wanted to stop at places of natural beauty within a two-hundred-mile radius of our already circuitous route.

But that was one of the fun things about being married to Chuck. He was always eager to discover natural beauty, and he avidly maintained ties with loved ones. Because of the bonds he'd made with distant relatives through his early genealogical research, we stayed at the homes of people we'd never met: some delightful Mormon cousins in Iowa, some Iowa relations of Chuck's mother, and his father's relatives in Minnesota. We saw the Black Hills, Mt. Rushmore, Devil's Tower, Little Big Horn, Glacier National Park, Missoula, Spokane, and the Cascade Mountains before arriving at our new home in the Pacific Northwest.

During the long hours of driving, I read to Chuck to pass the time. At first, I read the daily newspaper and articles from our AAA guides. When we visited Little Big Horn Battlefield in Montana, we bought a book called *Crazy Horse and Custer* by Stephen Ambrose, and I read that to him. We finished *Crazy Horse* while sitting on our new deck overlooking the Olympic Mountains.

After that, reading aloud became our morning ritual. Some of our favorite reads were Frank McCourt's *Angela's Ashes*, Mark Twain's *Adventures of Huckleberry Finn*, Ann Tyler's *Dinner at the Homesick Restaurant*, Erik Larson's *The Devil in the White City* (about the 1893 Chicago World's Fair), Harper Lee's *To Kill a Mockingbird*, John Steinbeck's *The Grapes of Wrath*, Homer's *The Iliad* and *The Odyssey*, and Juan Williams's *Eyes on the Prize*, a history of the early years of the civil rights movement.

Even as a nursing home resident with limited cognition, Chuck seemed to understand and follow the narrative of the books I read to him. At any rate, it was a comforting habit and a peaceful way to spend our afternoons. On days when he was able to go out, I would transfer him to the minivan, drive to a bakery for takeout lattes, and proceed to a spot with a water view where I would read to Chuck for as long as my voice held out or he stayed awake. Some days, I'd become lost in the author's words and slip into the illusion that we were once again sitting on our deck, and I was reading aloud to my husband as I'd done for years.

But then the light would fade or the cold would seep into the car, and it would be time to drive back to St. Thomas where I would get

Chuck settled in his room for dinner and kiss him good night. Then the route home was all too familiar. But entering our empty house and spending the night without him was not. I don't know how Chuck dealt with his solo evenings at St. Thomas. Did he ever cry? Did he feel alone or sad? I'm sure he did. But nothing could change that reality. We could either find new sources of joy and gratitude, or become bitter and angry about what life had dealt us. It was our choice. Chuck had usually led the way. Now it would be up to me.

*In an attempt to get a trumpeter swan to trumpet,*
*Chuck shows him a picture of a trumpeter swan.*

# 17

# Go Inward,
# Into Your Proper Darkness

Our son Teddy was born on November 1, which is All Saints' Day in the Christian calendar. Thirty years later when Ted participated in a yearlong Irish Studies program at The Evergreen State College, he discovered another ancient ritual celebrated on November 1: Samhain (SOW-en), or the Irish New Year.

Ted and I decided that on November 1, 2003, we would celebrate his birthday and Samhain at our house. In light of Chuck's new diagnosis, we hoped that this dual celebration would help our family begin a journey if not of healing, then of acceptance. Chuck's Irish roots (manifested in Ted's reddish-blond hair and beard) made Samhain a natural and appropriate family ritual.

The weather was perfect for Samhain: cold temperatures, gray skies, and the promise of rain. Ted brought his girlfriend Lela; Charles and his wife Hnoi joined us too. In the early afternoon, I brought Chuck home from St. Thomas Health & Rehab. Gathered together that day, our family observed some of the main activities of Samhain as the Irish have done for centuries. Ted's Irish Studies Professor, Sean Williams, had given her students a list of these activities, some with contemporary twists: *create a harvest feast, put your garden to bed for the winter and plant spring bulbs, trash unneeded computer files, throw away old candles and light new ones.* Those parts of the ancient rite would be simple to accomplish.

But there was one more, and I knew that this activity would be the hardest: *let go of the past and say hello to a new chapter of your life.*

I pushed Chuck's wheelchair into the kitchen and left him there to watch Ted assemble a thick, tomato-based broth flavored with basil and freshly squeezed orange juice. When I came back to check on them, the soup was simmering on the stove and the windows were steamed up. Chuck was cold so I wheeled him into the living room where Charles had started a fire.

I returned to the kitchen to make a loaf of Irish soda bread called *Aran donn*. The night before I'd combined oats and buttermilk in a bowl. Now I mixed in some flour, salt, and baking soda. I kneaded the heavy dough into a round and put it in the oven. Then I chopped apples, celery, and walnuts for an autumn salad, while Ted busied himself preparing "fairy cake" batter and pouring it into muffin tins.

While the bread and fairy cakes were baking, I woke Chuck so he could go outside with us. It took me several minutes to help him put on his winter coat, fur hat, and gloves. Ted maneuvered his father's wheelchair down the cement steps onto the front walk. From there Chuck watched as Ted, Lela, Hnoi, and I began to dig holes for daffodil, tulip, and hyacinth bulbs.

Juniper bushes had taken over the flower beds, and their roots refused to yield to the thrusts of our shovels. But eventually the earth flew apart in chunks, and we were able to pull out the tangled roots to make room for the bulbs. The wind chilled our bare hands, and Chuck asked to go back inside and sit by the fire. After I'd gotten him settled next to Charles, I returned to help rake Japanese maple leaves over the disturbed soil.

The night before I had burned all the old candles, thrown them away, and set new gold candles on our table. At the start of our harvest meal, Ted ladled tomato soup into bowls while Hnoi cut *Aran donn* into thick slices. I lit the candles and said a few words acknowledging our debt to the earth for our food. We spoke of those who had gone before us—my mother, my sister Carol, my grandmother, and Chuck's mother—all of whom died around this time.

By the time we'd finished dinner, Chuck was tired and ready to return to his small room at the facility. He and I were on solo journeys now. Though we interacted daily, nothing was the same.

*Let go of the past.*

When Chuck taught *Julius Caesar* to his high school students in Chicago, he would challenge them to cite three consecutive words from the play, and then he would identify the act and scene from which the words came, the character who spoke them, and to whom. A few weeks ago when we were filling out our absentee ballots, Chuck began to weep because he could not remember his last name.

*Say hello to a new chapter of your life.*

Professor Williams wrote these words about Samhain: "The past is gone and can never be revisited. The future, no matter how daunting it seems, lies ahead and should be approached with a child's innocent bewilderment, asking: What do I need to learn in this new chapter of my life? What do I have to offer? What do I fear? Why do I fear it? What can I learn from my fear? How can I go forward with strength and courage and wisdom? How can I love others and myself more completely?"

Her questions overwhelmed me, yet I was quietly confident that with patience and time, answers would come.

I thought about the bulbs we had planted, now lying deep in the earth. They would lie dormant throughout the winter. In the spring, their offshoots would tunnel through the black dirt, and then purple, yellow, and white blossoms would emerge into the sunlight. I wondered if I could ever mirror that process. At this point, when it took everything I had just to get through the day, I could identify with the bulbs buried in the darkness—but not with the spring flowers.

The family said their good-byes to Chuck as I transferred him into my car for the ride back to his new home. Though it was not quite five o'clock, the sun had already set on this bleak November 1, the first day of the Irish New Year. On this day, our Irish ancestors counsel us: "Go inward, into your proper darkness, and be a witness to your own growth."

# 18

# Three Men with Large Heads

I had been querying the social worker at St. Thomas about moving Chuck to a private room. In November his long-term care insurance claim had been accepted, and it now paid a large chunk of the nursing home bill. So I decided to add whatever extra money was needed for Chuck to have his all-important privacy. From the beginning, he had avoided other residents, and he refused to take part in any activities offered at the facility.

His first room had been a spacious double across the hall from the therapy room, and over the three months he resided there—with a break during the eleven days he lived at home—he had a series of three roommates. The first was Cecil, a wizened ninety-two-year-old, who gleefully told us that the huge black and yellow bruises on his arms and face were caused by his blood-thinning drug.

Chuck's second roommate was the bedridden Mr. Everly, whose wife and sister were constant presences in the room. When a nurse once asked him, "May I take your vitals?" Mr. Everly responded, "You can if I've got any." One day I arrived to find that Mr. Everly wasn't in his bed.

"They took him away in an ambulance," Chuck told me, and we never saw him again.

Chuck's third roommate was a middle-aged man named Mark, who had fallen during a diabetic coma and was rehabbing some broken bones. One morning I found Chuck sitting in the hallway wearing a leather hat and suede jacket that I didn't recognize because he'd taken them from Mark's closet. Mark laughed about it, but to me it was another disturbing indication of Chuck's confusion. At any rate, musical roommates did not seem to be in his best interests.

*Chuck exiting a nature reserve on the property of our sheep farmer friends in Akaroa, New Zealand—Chuck's favorite spot on earth.*

As it happened, a private room became available in mid-November. The social worker and I took Chuck to see it one morning. The room was on the front hallway with a street view and a large rhododendron bush outside the window. It contained a single hospital bed, a wooden wardrobe, a standard-issue bedside table, a padded armchair, and a private bathroom with toilet and sink.

"I like it," he said, and agreed to move that afternoon.

Of course, I was relieved and glad that he'd have his own room. But at the same time, my heart was breaking because I knew the rooms in the front hallway were reserved for "permanent residents."

Although he was still subject to institutional routines such as set mealtimes, Chuck was able to enjoy a semblance of privacy in his new room. He watched the programs he wanted without a second TV blaring from the other side of the privacy curtain. He could go to sleep at night without being awakened by someone else's snoring, wanderings, or emergencies. Whenever anyone left his new room, he would call out, "Shut the door!" Though his command sounded rude, I understood that being in charge of this small space gave Chuck a modicum of control over his life.

Over time we personalized Room 30 by adding three bulletin boards. These displayed snapshots of family and friends; posters of Martin Luther King Jr. and Akaroa, New Zealand (Chuck's favorite place in the world); a wall calendar on which I wrote his daily schedule; a rainbow "PEACE" flag his sister Judith sent from Italy; and drawings by Alex and Sharky. Two card tables held flower arrangements, jigsaw puzzles, a ceramic nightlight of Comiskey Park (Chuck remained a lifelong Chicago White Sox fan, although when we moved to Washington he shifted his baseball allegiances to the Seattle Mariners), a stack of letters and printed emails, his boom box, and the daily TV schedules I wrote out for him on yellow legal pads.

People entering Chuck's room for the first time often remarked that it was homier than other rooms. When he requested a recliner, I bought one with a control that lifted him from a sitting to a standing position. Then he never sat there. But the grandkids loved playing in it.

One afternoon when we were out driving, Chuck became noticeably tired and said, "I'd like to go home, please." I looked at him and waited. "My room," he clarified.

Even as Chuck began to settle into the nursing home, he insisted on eating all his meals alone in his room, shunning the common dining room. But one day a new aide wheeled him into the dining room for lunch. I'm sure Chuck protested, but apparently she didn't understand. When I arrived at 2:00, he told me, "I sat at a table with three men who had large heads. They did not speak." I was trying to envision these alien Humpty Dumpties when he added, "Those people are just waiting to die."

Later that afternoon I pushed him past the nursing station, which was surrounded by residents slumped in wheelchairs. Back in his room he told me in a clear voice, "Don't let this place prolong my life. I see those pathetic people in the hallway, and I'm afraid I might become one of them."

A few weeks later on another day when he was cognitively clear, I drove him to our favorite bakery. We sat at a table on the outdoor patio and worked on his Five Wishes document (see Appendix A): a living will that allows a person to specify his medical, personal, emotional, and spiritual wishes during his last days. With tears streaming down our cheeks, we read through the questions one by one and I filled in his answers. Chuck's responses that day gave me invaluable information about how he wanted his life to proceed from then on—and how he wanted it to end.

# 19

# Because I Can

Our marriage would last as long as Chuck and I had breath. But now, I needed to create a reasonably happy life apart from him. As Sue, Sharon, my doctor, and my friends and family had been telling me all along, as a caregiver I needed to take care of myself.

First, I hired people to do my least favorite chores: cleaning the house and mowing the lawn. Next, I bought hearing aids. I had a long-standing hearing loss, but had never done anything about it. Now that Lewy body dementia had rendered Chuck's voice so soft I could barely hear him, I finally bought the aids. These were baby steps, but each one made my life more manageable.

Another self-care issue involved my daily visits to the nursing home. I had not spent a day away from Chuck since his stroke five months earlier. But that November, an unexpected opportunity to get some respite presented itself. Our sister-in-law Clare—Chuck's brother's widow, who ran a ski lodge in Vermont—wrote to ask if she could spend Thanksgiving with us. She insisted that after the holiday I take a vacation, and she promised to spend time with Chuck while I was gone.

At first, I was afraid to leave him. What if he needed me? My assumption that his welfare depended on my presence was magical thinking. Once my therapist Sue helped me to see that, I accepted Clare's offer.

But where should I go? I considered several possibilities before choosing a condo-style resort on the Pacific Ocean. Driving to the coast meant that I wouldn't need a complicated itinerary with ferries or planes or trains, and I'd be close enough to rush home in case of an emergency.

I dreaded telling Chuck. But one afternoon a week before Thanksgiving, I screwed up my courage. When I told him I would be going away for a few days, he was lying on his bed. He listened carefully.

Then he said, "It will be good to see Clare. You should drive around that island. You always wanted to do that."

Before Chuck's stroke, I'd been planning a Vancouver Island itinerary for us. I knew that was what he meant and was amazed he'd managed to dredge up that memory.

"That's very kind of you," I said. "But that trip would take too long. I thought I'd just drive out to the coast. To Moclips."

"Have we ever been there?"

"I think we drove through there once, but we didn't stay overnight."

He was quiet for a few moments, and then he asked, "So, are you going to make any big decisions while you're away?"

I interpreted his question as: Are you in this marriage for the long haul—or are you planning to bail now that I'm sick?

"Big decisions?"

With a small smile, he said, "Like if you're going to shoot me."

I kissed his cheek. "No big decisions. I'm just taking a break."

I immediately regretted my word choice because "taking a break" wasn't possible for him. I knew that when I took to the road, he wouldn't be riding in the passenger seat as usual. He'd be lying in a nursing home bed, waiting for me to return.

Then he said matter-of-factly, "You don't ask me for advice anymore."

Surprised and a little amused, I asked, "Do you have some advice for me?"

He touched my hand. "Don't beat yourself up over Chuck. Chuck is fine."

He'd never referred to himself in the third person before, but that strange phrasing made his words feel like a blessing.

After Chuck had eaten his noontime Thanksgiving dinner at St. Thomas, he had no problem eating a second turkey dinner at home with the family later that afternoon. During our meal Clare suggested, "Why don't we go around the table and say what we're thankful for?"

Ben said, "I'm thankful we're the kind of family that doesn't go around the table saying what we're thankful for."

"Apparently we are," observed Charles.

"So what are you thankful for, Charles?" asked Ben. These kinds of scenes had played out between the two brothers many times, but lately they'd taken on a more playful tone. Both now worked in high-end computer jobs; both were bright and still a bit competitive.

"I'm thankful I live with Hnoi instead of you. What are *you* thankful for, Dad?"

Chuck glanced up from his turkey. "That I'm not at that Den of Iniquity."

After dinner, Ben and Ted drove their father back to the Den of Iniquity and got him settled in Room 30. Ted said that Chuck straightened a pile of papers on the card table and fluffed his pillows. Ben said, "It was like Dad was nesting." Chuck seemed to be settling in, and that made me feel better about taking my trip.

Two days after Thanksgiving, I kissed Chuck good-bye—first putting six of his sugar-free mocha puddings in the nursing home fridge and a stack of daily TV schedules on his card table. Armed with an NPR audiobook of autobiographical vignettes (good for my short attention span), I headed for the ocean feeling a combination of anxiety and anticipation. Oh, those conflicting feelings!

After driving for an hour, I came upon a nature reserve with trails that wound through fields and marshes along the Hood Canal. Only last May, Chuck and I had stopped there on our way to see Ted and Ben in Olympia. We'd decided to stretch our legs by taking a bird walk with our binoculars in the sanctuary. But Chuck had grown tired, so we cut the walk short. Should I have known then that something was wrong?

I chose not to walk through the reserve this time, but a little farther on I stopped at a state park to see if the salmon were spawning, as they usually did in November. Sure enough, dozens of chum had entered the shallow river from the canal. They struggled against the current, their last frantic moments spent depositing eggs on the gravel. Dead salmon lay in piles on the river bottom; they would be washed back into the canal or eaten by crows.

Back on the road, I turned off the audiobook and drove the next two hours in silence. I had a lot to ponder. What parts of our lives had Chuck and I lost forever? What parts were still salvageable? Everything had changed since June 18th. Now the future seemed like an endless stretch of time that had to be filled ... with what? Our life together could end tomorrow or in ten years—or twenty years. How should we live it?

Maybe Chuck was right. I did have some big decisions to make while I was away.

I checked into the resort a little after 2:00 p.m.—the time I would normally be arriving at St. Thomas. My large room had a king-size bed and a fireplace. I put away the milk and yogurt I'd bought for the mini-fridge to avoid eating breakfast at the resort's expensive restaurant. But I did call the restaurant to make a dinner reservation. Then I lay down in the huge bed on the left side, as usual, and took a rest.

The restaurant was perched on a bluff overlooking the Pacific Ocean where waves crashed and rolled on the wide beach below. I appeared there at 5:45 with a book in hand. The maître d' glanced over my shoulder and said, "Only one?"

During dinner, I wept because I had become one of those solitary women who read in restaurants. Crying felt like such hard work these days. That night in my room, I lit a pressed-wood log in the fireplace, and it exploded and set off the smoke alarm. If Chuck had been with me, we would have laughed. But I just opened the door and nervously flapped a towel until the smoke cleared and the blaring stopped.

The next day I walked the sandy beach for miles. Back at the resort, I swam in the indoor pool and had a massage. I ended up telling the chatty masseuse my story, which made her go silent. Afterward, she told me that regular massages would help release toxins from my body and reduce stress. "That's something you should do for yourself," she advised.

I continued journaling on my yellow pad. I thought about some myths I'd previously held as true, and came up with these new guidelines:

1. No one is responsible for anyone else's happiness.
2. You can't control certain parts of life.
3. You must take responsibility for your own life.
4. You must find the things that make you happy.

On my last morning I checked out, bought myself a red polar fleece jacket I'd been admiring in the gift shop, and drove a mile down the highway for a last walk on the beach.

I stood facing the ocean with my cold hands jammed into my pockets. With the sound of waves roaring in my ears, I wondered, *Why in God's name am I standing here alone? This is so unfair!*

I yelled at the ocean, "Why do *I* get to be here and he doesn't?"

After a few seconds, the words came back: "Because I can."

A few days after I'd returned from the coast, I wrote in my journal:

> *My thought at the moment is that it's a blessing to be able to take care of him. To ease him to wherever he's going. Not to complain about who will take care of me, but to accept that this is my life now. To accept it as a privilege, an act of love and compassion. Not to fight. Not to quibble or complain. Just to accept it.*

I knew I could not fix the brokenness that had descended into our lives, and with that realization came such sadness—and relief. And because I didn't have to be Superwoman any longer, I could spend a bit of time figuring out who Florrie was. I began with the certain knowledge that I had been sublimating my own needs for many years. Chuck had not asked me to do this. It had been my choice.

And it was going to change.

Our family returned to the island for Christmas, and again I felt embraced by their loving presence and spirit of fun. They all helped with meals (Isabel and James cooked about 200 waffles and twelve pounds of bacon over the course of four breakfasts), and our sons took turns making dinners and transporting their father to and from the Den of Iniquity. On Christmas Day, I dressed Chuck in the Santa suit that Isabel had sewn for him years ago, and he handed out the gifts, as was our tradition. Five-year-old Alex assisted him by reading the name tags. For four days we held a grand house party, but on the evening of the 28th, I found myself alone again in the big house.

On December 31, 2003, I concluded my journal titled, "Chuck's Stroke and Recovery" that I'd begun on June 18, "The Day Everything Changed." I was done reliving the past six months. I wanted to put all of that behind me. The last words I penned in my journal were these:

> *Good riddance to 2003. As if calendars had anything to do with anything. But seasons do. And now we are post-Solstice. Darkness seems to mean a lot to me now. This is the last day I will write on these yellow pages. I am, so to speak, turning a new page. I'm going to stick them in a bag and put them somewhere I can't find them. I'm done. Good night.*

6
___

*PASSAGES*

*1969–1989*

# 20

# We Are Nutmeggers

By January 2004, I'd been living by myself in our 3,900-square-foot home for over six months. During Washington winters, darkness descends around 4:00 p.m. and lasts until 8:00 a.m. When Chuck and I lived together, sixteen hours of darkness a day never bothered me. Now that I was alone, the dark brought on feelings of isolation and fear.

When we'd moved to our house in 1989, we hired Chuck's carpenter cousin to build two bedrooms and an office for me in the basement. I was now afraid to go down there at night, so Ben and Ted moved my computer and printer upstairs to Chuck's office. Though our neighbors lived fairly close by, I rarely saw lights from their houses (I looked). And when I turned on my upstairs lights I felt vulnerable, as if I were living inside a big fishbowl. But I was stuck. If I moved, it would be the final announcement to Chuck that he was never coming home. Preserving the illusion of his recovery might have been silly, but I didn't feel strong enough to address the issue. So I soldiered on in my dark house.

But I began to dream about moving to a smaller place where I would feel safer. If I could pull it off, it would be the first time in my life I'd lived alone. For the past thirty-five years, I'd lived with Chuck. And though Chicago had been the cradle of our young love, our married life began, unexpectedly, in Connecticut.

After his wife and children moved to Rockford, Illinois, in December of 1968, Chuck began toying with the idea of making a career change. He loved teaching, but he'd been pushed to the brink by a public school bureaucracy that treated students like commodities and heaped paperwork and restrictions on underpaid teachers. His meager salary meant that he had to augment his income by working weekends (teaching adult GED classes) and summer jobs (teaching summer school or cleaning toilets at Lake Michigan beaches).

Racial tensions in the city ran high, and relations with police were strained. One of his male students confided to Chuck that two policemen had forced him into their squad car and dropped him off in rival gang territory "to teach him a lesson." The boy made it home safely, but with an even stronger mistrust and fear of the police.

Chuck had lived his entire life in Chicago, but he was ready to leave. After my graduation, I was willing to go wherever he wanted to live. Pat and their children lived ninety-five miles away, so Chuck rarely saw Charles (10), Isabel (8), and Ben (4). He assumed correctly that Pat would be granted child custody, and if he was allowed to see his children only a few weeks a year, he didn't have to stay in Chicago.

Chuck had always dreamed of being a writer, so early in 1969 he began applying for jobs at educational publishing houses on the East Coast. A few companies flew him to New York for interviews, so we assumed he would end up in Manhattan. But when he visited American Education Publications in Middletown, Connecticut, he fell in love with the rolling green hills and took a job with the company that produced *My Weekly Reader*. He would be a writer for *You & Your World*, a classroom periodical with a circulation of 350,000, written for high school students who were reading at a third- to fifth-grade level—like many of his Chicago students. As soon as the 1968-69 school year ended, Chuck moved to Connecticut to begin his new job. He mailed me a card from Middletown on which he wrote:

> *We never part*
> *We never conclude a letter*
> *Without saying "peace."*
> *But you know*
> *You are my peace*
> *Without you there is no peace*
> *And I am your peace*

*And we are our Peace*
*And in that*
*God has greater glory.*

*Peace!*

For my graduation, Mom and Dad gave me $800 for a down payment on a light-blue 1969 Volkswagen Squareback. I named the car Vardaman after a boy in William Faulkner's novel, *As I Lay Dying*. (I had just taken my English comprehensive exams.) My college friend Gaylen and I squashed our belongings into the back of Vardaman, and two and a half days later I dropped Gaylen in Hartford, Connecticut, and made a beeline for Middletown.

When I pulled Vardaman into a parking space on Broad Street, it took me about five seconds to climb the stairs to Chuck's apartment. We had been apart for three weeks, and that seemed like a lifetime. That night he made me a dinner of meat loaf and apple pie. The next day I began job hunting, and a few weeks later I signed a contract to teach English at Middletown High School starting in September. With that, we had become official residents of Connecticut. Colloquially speaking, we were Nutmeggers! What a delicious adventure to live in a state where no one knew us!

That summer we listened to music—"Abraham, Martin and John," "Give Peace a Chance," "You Make Me So Very Happy"—on WESU, Wesleyan University's student-run radio station. We delighted in the small size of our new state, and Chuck convinced me we needed to explore Connecticut during the good weather. On weekends we swam in lakes at state parks, drove downriver to explore the seaports, and visited tourist sites like Devil's Hopyard and Gillette Castle. On July 20, we gazed up at the night sky from a campground in New Hampshire, filled with wonder that our countryman Neil Armstrong was at that moment walking on the moon.

Just before school started, we left the Broad Street apartment where Chuck had taught me to kill cockroaches by sneaking up on them with a rolled newspaper and flicking on the overhead light. We moved into a two-room cottage on a grassy hillside in Moodus, half an hour's drive downriver.

*Our first home in Moodus, Connecticut.*

Our cottage had once been part of a resort but was now privately owned. The area had been what Chuck called a "Poor Man's Poconos"—a summer playground for New Yorkers who wanted a cheap vacation in the country. A few resorts still operated, including the Grand View Lodge (which we called the "Mediocre View Lodge") across the street from our wee cottage. We hiked the meadows of the vacant resorts on weekends, Chuck with his binoculars and me with one of my mother's old Zeiss Ikon cameras. On weekdays we took the highway to work in Middletown and explored the back roads on our return. We got lost a few times, but we discovered every road eventually leads you home.

In mid-November, Chuck's divorce came through, and we made plans to marry the following weekend. There would be no church, no bridesmaids or ushers, no engraved invitations, no reception with formal dining and dancing at the country club—like the weddings my mother had planned for my sisters. I don't think it even crossed my mind that it might be a hardship for my parents to fly from Chicago to Connecticut on such short notice. I simply told them, "We're getting married on Sunday. Can you come?"

On Sunday, November 16, 1969, the sun shone on a clearing in the woods next to a waterfall in Moodus, Connecticut. Chuck and I had discovered this spot on our walks, and we wanted to share its beauty and sanctity with our loved ones. At last, it was our moment to shine and share the love we'd been holding in secret for the past year. I wore a simple blue and brown suit and a belted tan car coat; Chuck wore a turtleneck, a brown V-neck sweater, and a tweed sport coat.

*On November 16, 1969, Chuck and I celebrated our marriage*
*next to a waterfall in Moodus, Connecticut.*

Our guests parked their cars on the rural road and walked through snow-crusted grass to the clearing. My brother-in-law Bob held the arm of my frail mother while my father walked behind, filming with his Super 8 movie camera. Chuck's brother Stan and his two older children drove down from Vermont, while his wife Clare stayed home with their two little ones. Also attending were my sister Susie, my college friends Gaylen and Sarah, and Paul, a former student of Chuck's who was an intern at the nearby Goodspeed Opera House.

*My sister Susie and my parents attended our wedding.*

After Stan took a few photos of the two of us with the waterfall as backdrop, everyone formed a circle, and Chuck and I passed out copies of the marriage ceremony we had written. It included an excerpt from the Bible, a Navajo chant, and poems from Kahlil Gibran and e. e. cummings. We all read our parts aloud with Paul acting as leader.

I don't remember the cold. I don't remember the snow; Bob told me about it years later. I don't remember if I had a bridal bouquet. I don't remember what we did afterward, although we did have a celebratory dinner at the Manchester Inn.

What I do remember is relief that our long period of waiting was over. Our love had survived the hardships of the past year, and Chuck and I were now legally married.

The next day Chuck and I returned to work, and my parents flew home to Chicago. I knew they weren't happy about our marriage, but they loved me enough to come and be witnesses. We were grateful.

A few weeks later Mom and Dad mailed us a formal, engraved announcement of our marriage, which explained why we received wedding gifts from some of their kind friends. I viewed it as a compromise, maybe even an olive branch. It didn't matter. The painful conflict with my parents was over.

Many years later, my mother's best friend told me that Mom had initially refused to come to our wedding. My father reminded her that she'd already lost one daughter when Carol died three years earlier. Was she prepared to lose another? So Mom relented. Someone had to make the first move, and it turned out to be her. I now realize that my mother was trying to protect me from jumping into a relationship with quite a few odds against it. If only she could have lived long enough to see what a special marriage Chuck and I had. Then she would have known that her fears were unfounded.

On my first day back at school, I announced my new marital status by writing "Mrs. Munat" on the blackboard. With a small smile, I told my students, "This is what you should call me now."

A group of girls at the back of the classroom let out a collective, "Ooooohhhhh!"

Chuck announced his new status with a memo to his workmates:

To: My Special Ed Colleagues
From: Chuck Munat  *CEM*
Date: November 17, 1969
Subj: Good News

I am pleased to announce the appointment of Miss Florence Margaret Howe as my lawful wedded wife, effective November 16, 1969.

Florrie—a native of Winnetka, Illinois, and a graduate of Lawrence University in Appleton, Wisconsin—is an English teacher at Middletown High School. Her ambition (poor girl) is to be a professional writer.

Florrie looks forward to meeting those of you she has not yet met. Together we hope that our joy may brighten your Monday morning.

P.S.  I'll probably be a little late today.

# 21

# A Steaming Cauldron

A month after our wedding, we drove Vardaman back to Chicago to spend the Christmas holidays with Chuck's mother, my parents, and "the kids," as we called Charles, Isabel, and Ben. I had just quit teaching, which had been a questionable career choice for an under-confident introvert. I would soon be working in the promotion department at Wesleyan University Press, a much less stressful job.

Chuck's job continued to be stressful with a heavy writing workload and almost-daily deadlines, but he loved it. And he had good benefits, including four weeks' paid vacation. For the next three years, he would take off one week at Christmastime to see his children in Illinois and three weeks in the summer when he flew the kids from Illinois to Connecticut for a New England vacation with us.

The first summer we all crammed into the little cottage in Moodus. Chuck bought a Havahart trap, designed to humanely capture small animals without harming them. My mother used one to trap squirrels that ate the sunflower seeds from her birdfeeders, and then she drove any captive critters to a forest preserve and released them. The kids baited our trap with peanut butter and set it out near the resort's old swimming pool, now home to an army of frogs and a lot of muck.

Next morning we hurried outside, eager to see what they'd caught—a raccoon, a rabbit, or a squirrel? To the kids' delight, the trap contained one sleepy skunk. Chuck opened the trap door with the longest stick he could find, and the nocturnal varmint waddled off into the woods.

Not long after the kids returned to Rockford, Chuck and I bought our first home, a two-bedroom ranch house farther downriver in East Haddam. The kids joined us there the next two summers.

Growing up, I didn't have much exposure to young children. Because I didn't have younger siblings and hadn't even done much babysitting, I felt unsure about how to treat Charles, Isabel, and Ben. All three had strong personalities and, unlike my sisters and me, they often settled disputes by argument. Occasionally, Charles and Ben would launch into fistfights that made my childhood look like something out of *Little Women* (which it probably was).

So during our summers together, I stayed in the background and cooked the meals. I let Chuck make the decisions about where to go and what to do. The kids called me "Florrie" and rarely gave me a hard time, though our engagement was minimal. My preference back then would have been for Chuck and me to spend our vacations alone. But I understood that he and his children needed time together, and I did have him to myself the other forty-eight weeks of the year. Chuck picked up on my reluctance to discipline the kids and played the father role with authority. But his love for all of us, plus his zany sense of humor, set the stage for a lot of fun.

*Charles (11), Isabel (9), and Ben (5) about to board their plane after spending three weeks with Chuck and me in Connecticut in the summer of 1970.*

Summer vacations were filled with activities. We camped on the Appalachian Trail in Vermont and at Nickerson State Park on Cape Cod. The kids renamed it "Tickerson State Park" after some deer ticks (the relatively harmless kind) found their way into our tents and onto our skin. We showed the kids New York City and Boston. We toured Plimoth Plantation, Sturbridge Village, Mystic Seaport, and the Hartford Zoo. We walked the greens at Lexington and Concord where Chuck entertained us with Revolutionary War stories; we experienced Civil War reenactments and listened to fife & drum corps. We attended town fairs where Nutmeggers held competitions for the tastiest jam, the strongest horse team, the most elegant quilt, the handsomest lop-eared rabbit, and the fattest baby.

*In 1980, a large group of Munats gathered for Thanksgiving at the White Pine Lodge in Landgrove, Vermont. Very top: Ben Munat. Top row: Clare Munat, Mary Munat, "Tall" Stan Munat, Daniel Lenggenhager (Swiss AFS student). Middle row: Judith Munat, Stan Munat, Florrie Munat, Maggi Munat, Isabel Munat, James Travers (AFS student from New Zealand), Barbara Peake (James's fiancée). On the ground: Alex Costa (Judith's son), Teddy Munat, Jon Munat, and Blue the dog.*

Chuck's older brother Stan and his wife Clare owned a ski lodge in rural southern Vermont. We spent many days with their family at the White Pine Lodge, where our kids and their four cousins roamed the woods, swam in the pond, and performed skits and songs—much to the delight of the adults. Stan was a Korean War vet, a *summa cum laude* philosophy major at the University of Illinois, and a pioneer in the new field of computer science. He'd worked in New York City for several years and then ditched his corporate job and bought the Vermont lodge that he and Clare ran as a family operation. Clare had a master's degree in anthropology from NYU and traveled to Manhattan for concerts and lectures.

I found them to be smart, funny, cosmopolitan, Bohemian, and kind. During our times at their lodge, we spent hours watching movies from Stan's esoteric video collection that introduced me to a whole new world of cinema. We happily imbibed Stan's cocktails and ate Clare's gourmet dinners while the seven kids entertained themselves. Going to Vermont was like going on vacation with your best friends.

Spending time with Chuck's kids was fine, but as a young woman I longed to have my own children. Chuck and I discussed it, but half his paycheck was earmarked for child support. After two years with both of us working and saving, plus a small inheritance I received from my grandmother, our finances finally reached the point where we could afford a child, and I became pregnant early in 1971.

During my pregnancy, Chuck and I attended Lamaze classes, which introduced us to other couples whose babies were due around the same time as ours, and we made some good friends. Besides learning breathing techniques to use during labor and delivery, our Lamaze coach taught us the basic philosophy of natural childbirth: mothers should avoid anesthesia because its sedating effects would be transmitted to the unborn children. That all sounded great, so I signed on for natural childbirth. But I'd never had a labor pain, so what did I know?

Two months before my due date, I quit my job at Wesleyan Press. While I waited at home, I decorated the nursery walls with framed felt replicas of story characters: Winnie-the-Pooh, Piglet, Babar the elephant, and the Little Prince. We borrowed a crib and bassinet, and my mother arranged for a diaper service.

My labor began on Halloween day, but then stopped until we'd gone to bed—when it began again with a vengeance. In my self-effacing manner, I let Chuck sleep and tiptoed to the living room sofa. Lying there, I timed my contractions and slept in fifteen-minute intervals between labor pains.

Chuck discovered me at 6:00 a.m. He stood next to the couch in his pajamas and looked at me incredulously. "How long have you been here?"

"Since about 10:30 last night."

He picked up my notepad. "Your contractions are six minutes apart? We need to get to the hospital!"

"You think so? Okay, would you call the doctor? We're supposed to let him know when we're on the way."

He turned toward the kitchen to get the phone. "Where's his number?"

"Um, I forgot to write it down. Can you look it up?"

"Yeah, sure. What's his name?"

"Cerritelli."

A minute later, Chuck appeared in the kitchen door with the phone book in his hand. "How do you spell it?"

"C-E-R-"

"Oh, no wonder. I was looking under S."

So far, our parenthood had been pretty disorganized.

Chuck put my small suitcase into the back of Vardaman, and we headed off to the hospital, twenty miles away. The shortcut began with a dirt road near our house. Chuck asked me if it would be okay to go that way as opposed to the paved street alternative, and I said yes—because I wasn't having a contraction at the moment. But as soon as he started driving, a contraction arrived and I yelped each time he drove over a rut, all the way to the East Haddam Bridge. After the bridge, it was smooth sailing on the highway to Middletown.

*Chuck and I welcomed baby Teddy in November 1971.*

On November 1, 1971, at 12:29 p.m., our son Edward Colahan Munat was born. *Edward* for my father, grandfather, and great-grandfather, all named Edward Cole Howe; and *Colahan* for Chuck's mother, née Margaret Katherine Colahan. We called the baby "Teddy."

Sweaty and exhausted after fourteen hours of labor, I felt overwhelmed by joy and awe for the tiny boy I clasped to my chest. He was a miraculous mixture of Chuck and me, except for his inexplicable red hair. Thanks to the entreaties and encouragement of my Lamaze coach and Chuck, I managed to get through the birth without anesthetic. Barely.

Chuck and I made local hospital history in three categories. First, Chuck was one of the first fathers allowed in the delivery room to witness the birth of his child. Second, he was *the* first father allowed to bring a camera into the delivery room. And third, my roommate and I became the first mothers whose babies stayed in the room with us, rather than being carried off to the nursery after feedings. The times were definitely a-changin'!

Back at work, Chuck wrote an article for "You & Your World" about a controversial soap product that was used to wash newborns at the time. He illustrated the article with his photo of Dr. Cerritelli holding up newborn baby Teddy.

In a grand gesture of reconciliation, my mother flew out to spend a week with us after Teddy's birth. Though our prickly relationship resurfaced (assisted by my postpartum depression), I appreciated that she made the effort to see her newest grandchild.

During Christmas vacation, Chuck and I drove Vardaman to Chicago for the second year in a row so the kids could meet their one-month-old brother. The threesome stared at him as he slept, awed by his tiny fingers and toes. When they visited Connecticut the following summer, eight-month-old Teddy had become more interactive. Whatever conflicting emotions they harbored about their mostly absent father and their quiet stepmother, Charles and Isabel and Ben found it easy to focus their affection on their baby brother, who they toted around like a Raggedy Andy doll, much to Teddy's delight.

*In 1971, Chuck and I returned to Chicago to spend Christmas vacation with his three children—Isabel, Ben, and Charles.*

*Two months after Teddy's birth, Chuck and I open Christmas presents at my parents' home in suburban Chicago.*

That summer of 1972, the kids' visit began with a weeklong stay at Stan and Clare's ski lodge in the cool Green Mountains. Then the six of us got into our Volkswagen camper van and descended into the Connecticut River Valley where ninety-five-degree temperatures and ninety-five percent humidity made it feel like we'd been dropped into a steaming cauldron. Back in East Haddam, our daily routine was to pack a picnic lunch and drive to the Moodus Reservoir (near our wedding waterfall) where the cool water and a breeze brought some relief from the hot, humid weather.

As the kids' vacation days dwindled, Chuck arranged a surprise for their return flight to Chicago. All three children were interested in airplanes, and the new Boeing 747—the largest jet ever flown—had just come into operation. None of these jets flew in and out of Bradley Field in Connecticut. So Chuck and I planned to drive the kids to Boston where they would board a brand-new 747.

Two days before their departure, Chuck dropped Teddy and me at home after our daily swim at the reservoir. Then he drove the kids to Middletown to shop for school clothes.

The house was unbearably hot so I plopped Teddy into the bathtub. Then, tempted by the cool water, I joined him. I'd just settled into the tub when the phone rang. I wrapped Teddy and me in a bath towel, hurried to the kitchen, and grabbed the phone. As the baby and I dripped onto the linoleum, a woman's voice said, "I'm calling from a hospital in Sycamore, Illinois, with regard to Patricia Munat. Do you know her?"

"Yes, I do. I'm sorry, who did you say this is?"

"I'm a nurse. Calling from a hospital in Illinois. Your phone number was in her wallet. May I ask how you know her?"

"I'm married to her husband. Her ex-husband, I mean."

"Is he home? I need to speak to him."

"He's not here now, but he'll be back in an hour or two. Can I take a message?" She paused, and I shifted Teddy to my other hip, both of us still slippery from the bathwater. "Did Pat … is she sick?"

"Patricia was in an automobile accident this afternoon."

"Oh. Is she all right?" Teddy was struggling to get down so I set him on the floor, and he crawled toward a pile of plastic Bristle Blocks.

"Well, it was a serious accident. Her car was hit by a truck, and she was brought in by ambulance. They worked for almost two hours and did everything they could." I waited for her next words. "But she died one hour ago."

I pulled the towel more tightly around my shoulders and watched Teddy stack a blue block on top of a red one. "Are you sure? That it was Pat, I mean. Could there have been some mistake?"

"I'm sorry. Patricia is dead. Just to make sure our records are correct, may I ask again: what is your name and your relationship to the deceased?"

"The deceased? Well, I'm married to … I'm her children's step-mother."

After I set the phone down, I lowered myself onto the floor and watched Teddy play. I was twenty-five years old. Eight months ago I had no children. Now I had four: thirteen-year-old Charles, eleven-year-old Isabel, seven-year-old Ben, and eight-month-old Teddy. Chuck and the kids would be home soon, and I'd have to tell him what the nurse told me. And then he would have to tell the children.

I picked up Teddy who cried out when I separated him from his blocks. I carried him wailing into the nursery, and comforted him with his favorite stuffed dog while I put a diaper on him and dressed him in clean clothes. Pat had loved her children and must have known how to comfort them too. How could I ever replace her?

# 22

# Our Brady Bunch Days

After Pat's death, Chuck and the kids and I wrestled with the workings of our new family. A therapist would have helped a great deal, but back in 1972 it never occurred to us to engage professional help, nor did anyone else suggest it. But none of us mistook our transition pains for the true tragedy: the sudden death of the children's mother at age thirty-seven.

Chuck and I flew with the four children to Chicago. Chuck and Leon (Chuck and Pat's good friend, and Charles's godfather) drove Charles, Isabel, and Ben to their mother's funeral in Rockford, while I waited with Teddy at my parents' house eighty miles away. Then our new family of six flew back to Connecticut.

Chuck had to return to work in Middletown, leaving the children and me marooned at our little house in the boondocks for five weeks until school started. I knew the kids had experienced a terrible loss and wanted to help them through their grief. But I felt overwhelmed by my own emotions and the logistics of suddenly coping with four young children.

Being Teddy's mother felt natural to me. But my knowledge of Charles, Isabel, and Ben was limited, gleaned only from our Christmas visits and three summer vacations. What was their favorite music? What were their dreams? What frightened them? I didn't know. As paterfamilias, Chuck tried to anticipate and handle everyone's needs while holding down a demanding job to support the six of us. The thought must have crossed his mind that I might take Teddy and leave. I admit that exit strategy did occur to me, but only as a fleeting wish for simpler days. Leaving was never an option. But challenges abounded as we each processed our own grief—while struggling to figure out what we might become together.

*One month after the death of the children's mother Pat, the six of us visited
my sister Susie's family at their cottage in the Berkshires.
My mother, Carol Howe, took this photo of us with my father.*

Chuck and I had chosen to live in East Haddam for its rural beauty,
without a thought for the quality of its schools. But that autumn as we
scoured central Connecticut for a larger home, our top priority became
finding a place with an excellent school system. We had hoped to move
before the school year started, but it took us until late October to find
a brown-and-white, two-story house secluded on an acre-and-a-half lot
in Middletown. We moved in a few days before Thanksgiving. Each of
the three older children had their own bedroom, and Teddy slept in a
nursery that was part of our master suite. From the back door, we could
walk to a forest with a creek. Our new home was seven miles from
Chuck's office and Charles and Isabel's new schools. Ben's elementary
school was located two miles down the road.

Right away I phoned my mother to tell her about our new house.
Recovering from surgery at Evanston Hospital, she said, "I'm looking
forward to seeing it."

Three days later, on Thanksgiving morning, I telephoned the hospital again to inquire about Mom. A disembodied female voice informed me, "The patient expired at 5:15 this morning." I went back to bed and cried while Chuck held me and chastised the woman for her tactless, callous words. Now I was motherless too—just like the kids.

Chuck and I were grateful to the friends who stayed with our children while we flew to Chicago for Mom's funeral. My father was magnanimous in his grief, welcoming me back to the home where I'd grown up and making sure I was surviving my new motherhood. I assured him I was fine, though inwardly I felt depressed and overwhelmed by the future.

But it's impossible to stay down when you're married to a man who wakes up singing, "My Lord, what a morning! My Lord, what a morning, when the stars begin to fall!" And who tells you you're the most wonderful thing that's ever happened to him—and that together you're going to get through this. And when he sees that you're sad, he hands you his handkerchief and quotes a line from a favorite sonnet: "But dearer far than all surmise are sudden teardrops in your eyes."

Two years after Pat died, I legally adopted her children, who had started calling me "Mom" a few months after her death. It would take me months, years maybe, to become close to Charles, Isabel, and Ben—and they to me. Of course, I could never replace Pat. But I tried to become my own version of their mother. Meanwhile, Chuck and his children had their own challenge: after four years of separation, they needed to reestablish full-time father-child relationships. Ironically, one event that helped us come together was the addition of another family member.

One night in the spring of 1974, Chuck called to order one of our notorious "Family Conferences." Chuck invented these dinnertime sessions to give everyone a chance to air grievances, ask questions, and address anything confusing or annoying. But Family Conferences often deteriorated into strenuous arguments, usually between Chuck and Charles. Charles was a lean fifteen-year-old with long brown hair and wire-rimmed glasses, a brilliant thinker who seemed to enjoy exercising his debating skills.

When the wrangling began, Teddy, a blond toddler, would invert his salad bowl over his head and slip under the dining room table. Isabel, who hated disagreements of any kind, would stand it as long as she could and then dash to her bedroom in tears. Third-grader Ben would take advantage of the distraction to feed unwanted parts of his dinner to Charlie the cat. Since my goal in life was to resolve every argument I encountered, I would stick around trying to make peace between the combatants, and when that proved impossible, I would go to Isabel's room to comfort her.

On this particular night, Chuck called the Family Conference to order and asked if anyone had anything to bring up. Ben said, "Whose week is it to feed Charlie? I did it last week so it's not mine!"

"It's my week, Ben," said Isabel. "You just watched me put Friskies in his bowl in the kitchen, nutty buddy!"

Ben stared morosely at his plate. His freckles and brown bangs reminded me of Huck Finn. He said, "Bobby Frederick throws up whenever he eats meat loaf. I can't eat this."

"I'm sorry you don't like meat loaf, Ben," I said, "but I'm not making separate dinners for everyone. Just eat what you can."

"Who's making dinner this Thursday?" Isabel asked.

"I think it's Charles's turn," I said.

"Yep, it is," said Charles. "We're having spaghetti."

"Again?" said Isabel.

"Wait, I was going to make spaghetti on my Thursday!" objected Ben.

"Make tuna casserole," Charles said. "Hey, did you notice that every time we use the electric can opener, Charlie runs into the kitchen because he thinks someone's opening a can of tuna?"

This made Ben laugh, and then Teddy laughed because he imitated everything that Ben did.

Chuck said, "Okay, next item. Who left the kettle on the burner until it melted?" He held up a silver ingot as big as a poker chip. "Exhibit One."

"Uh, that would be me." I half-raised my hand. "I put the kettle on and forgot it. I'll buy another one at Calder's tomorrow. One with a whistle." Chuck laughed his belly laugh, and then we all laughed. This was unusual. No arguments?

"Anything else?" Chuck asked.

Charles said, "Yeah, Dad. I think it's tyrannical that you make us pay ten percent of the electric bill. What is that? Some kind of economics lesson?" He and Chuck sat at opposite ends of the table eyeing one another.

*Here we go*, I thought.

Chuck began his standard answer whenever this topic came up. "Mom and I give each of you a generous allowance, much more than any of your friends get. And out of that we expect you to help pay some household expenses like one-tenth of the electric bill, your long-distance phone calls—"

Charles was waving his hand. "Never mind, never mind. I've heard your rationalizations, and they're unconvincing. The fact is you're using a negative—taking away our money—to achieve a positive. Or what you think is a positive result: lowering your bills."

Chuck said, "No, the result is that we use less electricity, which is good for the environment. And you learn that if you make a phone call, you pay for that phone call—"

Charles smacked the table with the palms of his hands. "And it's punitive to charge us a dollar—just because we don't have time to make our beds before school!"

Charlie the cat scurried into the kitchen with a piece of meat loaf in his mouth.

Chuck started to respond, but Charles interrupted again. "Anyway, I've got something more important to talk about. At the AFS club meeting today, Leila—she's the president—said we need families to host foreign exchange students next year. I thought that sounded cool so I said we would. But she says I have to ask my family first."

Isabel said, "Charles has a crush on Leila, that's why he volunteered. But it's a cool idea, even if it did come from him. I'd love to host a foreign student."

"Yeah," Ben agreed. "I'd like to have a brother who's not so mean. Remember when Charles was in the bathroom and he told me to go downstairs and stand under the laundry chute and look up? So I did, and he dropped a bar of soap down the chute—and it hit me in the eye!"

Charles rolled his eyes. "It was wrapped in a washcloth. It couldn't have hurt."

"But it did!" Ben's lower lip quivered. "I almost got a bruise!"

"We dealt with that when it happened, Ben," said Chuck. "And Charles was grounded for three nights."

"Oh, big deal," said Ben. "When you ground him, he just climbs out his bedroom window and goes and meets his friends."

"Shut up, Ben," said Charles.

"What?" Chuck looked at Charles. "What's he talking about?"

Ignoring the question, Charles continued. "Next year I'll be a sophomore and Isabel will be a freshman, so there'd be two of us to help our AFS student with school stuff. He'll be a senior so we won't be in the same classes, which is good. I've got bunk beds, so that solves the problem of where he'll sleep. But it also means we'll have to host a boy, unfortunately."

I was thinking about the AFS students I'd known in high school, and the idea of hosting appealed to me. But could we really handle one more child?

"All right," said Chuck. "Charles, you and I will deal with the window issue later. As for hosting an AFS student, it sounds good to me. Are you sure about sharing your bedroom though? You won't know anything about this boy until he gets here."

"As long as he likes the same kind of music I do and doesn't try to change the radio station, we'll be fine."

Isabel said, "Whoever the AFS kid is, I'll bet he doesn't read encyclopedias. Dad, did you know the kids in the neighborhood call Charles 'Brit'? It's short for *Britannica*."

Charles smirked. "They're just jealous."

"What volume are you on now?" she asked.

"D to F," Charles said. "More specifically, Delusions to Freemason."

Chuck turned to me. "Florrie, you haven't said much. What do you think about hosting an AFS student? If you don't want to, we won't. It'll be more work for you especially."

I shrugged. "Well, we've got six. I guess it won't make much difference if we have seven."

"Are you sure?" Chuck lifted his eyebrows, and I nodded. "Okay, it sounds like we'll move ahead with this."

Isabel said, "Nobody asked Teddy." She tickled her little brother's chin, making him giggle. "What do you think? Do you want another brother?" Teddy made a face and laughed.

Ben said, "We're going to be just like *The Brady Bunch*!"

Well, that might be a stretch. Granted, my name *is* Florence—same as the actress Florence Henderson, who played *The Brady Bunch* stepmother—but to me that's where the resemblance ended.

We all helped write our host family application, which was accepted by Middletown's adult AFS club. And in August of 1974, seventeen-year-old James Travers of Blenheim, New Zealand, became our AFS son/brother and the seventh member of the new Munat family. Demonstrating typical Kiwi hospitality, James quickly adapted to our makeshift family—except for his dislike of root beer, his puzzlement over American football rules, and one other thing. As it turned out, James and Charles did *not* like the same music or the same radio station, and they most definitely did not like sharing the same bedroom.

One evening that autumn while Chuck and I were preparing for bed, James appeared in our doorway and casually asked, "Mom and Dad, would it be all right if I moved my mattress downstairs to the laundry room and slept there?"

We got the message. Our AFS year would pass more peacefully if each boy had his own bedroom. So James and our dear friend Leo spent several weekends finishing a room in the basement—installing framing and sheetrock, painting, carpeting, and putting in baseboard heating. We took the bunk beds apart, creating two singles, and James moved his possessions into his new bedroom in December. We gave him a radio for Christmas, and all was well.

*James Travers, our AFS exchange student, ready for his senior prom at Middletown High School in 1975.*

In ways we never fully understood, adding a stranger to our family helped us heal. James was outgoing, inclusive, and kind. Our family adored him, as did everyone in the adult and student AFS clubs. He assumed the role of villainous Simon Darkway in the high school melodrama, and he played varsity tennis. Like our kids, he loved aeronautics, and he helped them wash private jets at an AFS fundraiser. And James was a marvelous AFS representative. When interviewed for the school and local newspapers, he graciously answered questions about New Zealand and his time in Middletown.

When his AFS year ended and James had to return to New Zealand, we were devastated. But over the years, the Munat and Travers families strengthened their ties. Two years after James left, his parents came and stayed with us for a week. Later, his sister Mary and niece Charlotte came for a visit.

*Our local newspaper reported the return of James Travers, our exchange student from New Zealand, and his fiancée Barbara in December 1980. At the time our family was hosting Daniel Lenggenhager, an AFS student from Switzerland. From left: Chuck (45), Daniel (18), Barbara (20), James (23), Florrie (33), Ted (9) and Ben (15).*

In 1980 James brought his fiancée to Middletown, and we were almost as smitten with Barbara as he was. At Christmastime in 1981, Chuck, Teddy, and I made our first trip to New Zealand for James and Barbara's wedding. So began our love affair with New Zealand, which led to five more trips to visit our beloved Kiwis and explore their homeland. During those visits, Chuck and I did some traveling around the country, but most of our time was spent camped out at Barbara and James's Wellington home, where their three children—Spencer, Elliot, and Brittany—called us "Grandma and Grandpa Munat." It took years for the Travers children to question why they had three sets of grandparents.

*In turn, Chuck and I were photographed by the* Marlborough Express
*in Blenheim, New Zealand, in 1990.*

While our children were attending Middletown High School, we hosted three other exchange students: Daniel Lenggenhager from Switzerland, Siri Ostman from Sweden, and David Thompson from Barbados. Isabel spent a summer with an AFS host family in Norway, and Ben spent a full AFS year in Madrid. Chuck and I stayed steadily involved with the adult AFS Club and consequently, we got to know many host families and foreign students.

During our Middletown years, Chuck was promoted from staff writer to editor of *You & Your World*, and he continued to teach 350,000 teenagers about current events, finding jobs, and handling money. When a large corporation bought the company, their newly hired managers—"bean counters," as Chuck called them—decided to raise subscription rates. As a result, Chuck's beloved *You & Your World* lost eight percent of its readership. But increased rates meant increased profits, and the bean counters threw a party to celebrate. Chuck boycotted the party, staying in his office to mourn the loss of 28,000 readers. His conflict with the powers that be was nothing new, but it eventually led to his being fired. He then found a job he loved teaching communication skills to African American and Hispanic pre-nursing students at Greater Hartford Community College.

*Chuck had a deep affection for all of his students. Here he is with the Greater Hartford Community College pre-nursing program graduates in 1985.*

Once Teddy started school, I wrote and published three nonfiction books and several articles. Later I earned a master's degree in library science and took a job as a reference librarian in Middletown.

Although we both loved our jobs, Chuck and I decided that we would embark on a new chapter of our lives when Ted graduated from high school. In the 1970s, Chuck had been invited on an editors' tour of the Pacific Northwest and loved it. After an exploratory visit to Washington and Oregon in 1988, we decided to move to Bainbridge Island. A few days after Ted's graduation in 1989, we headed for Washington. And with that, our Brady Bunch days came to an end.

# 23

# "Best Ever" Birthday

Below is an excerpt from *Us & Our World*, Chuck's family newsletter in which he refers to himself as "Dad Munat."

**DAD HAS 'BEST EVER' BIRTHDAY**
*by Chuck Munat—June 1992*

Bainbridge Island, Washington, USA, 25 Apr—*Today was Dad Munat's 58th birthday, and, without a doubt, it turned out to be very special. There was no big celebration. He and Mom spent the afternoon and evening in Seattle taking in a play and a movie. And none of the four children were home for the occasion—not in body anyway. But they were there in spirit. Each decided it was time to tell the old man what they thought of him, and tell it they did. Three wrote letters. The fourth left a phone message. Three chose prose. One tried poetry. They all waxed poetic. Here is a montage of excerpts from the four messages:*

> *"I love you as much as it is possible for one human being to love another, and … I respect you both as a father and as a fellow-traveler in life, and … I treasure my relationship with you beyond my ability to express it in words."*

> *"I learned from your tears in April of '68 that prejudice is hurtful and wrong."*

*"You taught me what so few white people seem to be able to do: have compassion for the oppressed while never seeing them as pathetic and helpless or patronizing them in any way."*

*"I wanted to tell you that I was thinking the other day... 'Gee, this fathering stuff isn't very easy after all.' And I think you did a pretty good job of it. So that's my mushy birthday wish to you."*

*"I grew and you hung back—pointing to a road—yet letting me walk alone—knowing the most valuable knowledge is learned through pain. You gave strength and accepted weakness. Shared joy and despair— coaxing me from doubt into hope. Molding me into an adult and giving me the credit... I love you with all my heart!"*

*"I've come to consider myself extremely lucky to not only have a father who is a decent man, but one who is a hero to me. I don't mean hero in the silly 'I wanna be a plumber just like my daddy' sense. I mean that when I think of what is good, right, and beautiful to me, I can point to you as a person who represents it all."*

*"...I learned... from you... such qualities as respect for the rights of other human beings, an appreciation for human dignity, a sense of the preciousness of life, a desire for justice, tolerance for others and their beliefs, a love of literature and the arts, an insatiable curiosity for how things work, a stubborn unwillingness to go against my ethical and moral beliefs, a feeling of awe at the beauty and complexity of life, a desire to preserve and nurture the planet and its inhabitants (human and otherwise), and so much more."*

*"Arms that gave a push—and sent me rolling on two wheels—across a vacant lot in Chicago. Hands that clapped in triumph at my first solo ride."*

*So what did Dad think of this sudden outpouring of adulation? "Well, I must admit," he tells U&OW, "that my first thought was that I had some incurable disease that no one was telling me about! But Florrie assures me that that is not so. My second thought is simply, 'Wow! What a precious honor. What a humbling experience! It's my best birthday ever, no doubt." Poor Dad was so dazed he didn't even notice the split infinitive. [See above: "... to not only have a father ... "]*

# TURN ON THE HURRICANE
## 2004

# 24

# Blue Clothes

Seven months had passed since Chuck's stroke. He almost always knew my name, and though he couldn't always express himself clearly, he knew who he was and where he was. But sometimes he was confused and spoke hardly at all. And then on rare days, he was almost his old self again. I was beginning to understand the meaning of the LBD symptom called "fluctuating cognition."

The nursing home's weekly menu provided me with a good litmus test of how well Chuck's brain was functioning. When I read aloud the two entrées for each day, if he made his choice quickly I knew his cognition was good. If he hesitated for long periods or asked a question like, "What *is* a pork chop?" I knew that menu selection would have to wait.

One afternoon, our neighbors Doug and Pipper stopped by St. Thomas. When they entered his room, Chuck called out from his wheelchair, "Well, look who's here!" The four of us had a lovely conversation that included reliving some bird-watching moments that Chuck and Doug had shared on a trip to Puerto Vallarta, Mexico.

"Chuck, do you remember that rare parrot we spotted?" Doug asked.

Chuck replied, "Yes, we saw it when we were eating lunch up in the hills."

"At a villa that belonged to John Huston," Pipper added brightly.

"Huston filmed *Night of the Iguana* down there," said Doug.

Chuck said, "His statue was at the end of the island with all the vendors."

I'm sure it was my imagination, but I felt like Doug and Pipper were glancing at me as if to say, "Dementia? He's the same old Chuck! Why are you keeping him here?"

Fortunately, I'd read some comments by other caregivers on the Lewy Body Dementia Association's website. Some of them had described similar moments when their loved ones functioned at a surprisingly high level, only to regress later. One woman had taken her husband to church where he gave an impassioned speech that was greeted with applause. But back at home afterward, she found him hiding in a closet. The caregivers had a name for this phenomenon: *Showtime*. And as they said, *Showtime* was inevitably followed by *Downtime*.

Predictably, Doug and Pipper weren't in Chuck's room the next day when he asked me to bring him his geothermal hat and lunch pail and became upset when I couldn't find those nonexistent items. Our neighbors also missed the day after that, when Chuck experienced what his nurse charted as "ten minutes of unresponsiveness."

And Chuck's hallucinations continued.

In addition to hiding in a foxhole and meeting Hitler, he told me that "a guy from Detroit, a lieutenant colonel in the Marines" had arrived the night before to recruit Chuck for a secret mission. During some of these "dreams," Chuck paced his room and fell. Over a three-year period, I recorded twenty-eight falls, and those were only the ones we knew about.

Chuck also experienced delusions, some of which were elaborate. One day in January 2004, I entered Room 30 and found him working on a children's jigsaw puzzle. Although he was still in his pajamas at 2:00 p.m., he looked very normal that day—legs crossed, holding a puzzle piece in his hand while studying the pieces on the card table. Classical music played on his radio. I sat down and noticed a pile of clothes next to his wardrobe.

"Why are those clothes on the floor?" I asked.

He looked at me as though I had failed to grasp the simplest concept. "They're blue." He returned his attention to the puzzle.

I turned up my hearing aids. "They're what?"

"They're blue!" he repeated more loudly.

"So ... what's wrong with blue clothes?"

He spoke with exasperation. "You can't wear blue if you're in the Nazi Army!"

"But you're not in the Nazi Army."

"Do you mean to tell me this place is not owned by the Nazi Army?"

"As far as I know, it's owned by a corporation in Milwaukee."

He looked abashed, but he accepted my explanation. "I suppose those will have to be washed," he said, looking balefully at the pile. "Since they've been sitting on the floor."

Chuck's cognitive confusion seemed to be taking him further and further away from me. Sue had been insisting that I deserved to have an independent life, and Chuck's decline motivated me to explore that possibility. In the past few months, I'd started attending a welcoming, progressive church, and I shared my story with new friends there. I rejoined my monthly book group and Circle Babes, my weekly women's support group. I walked at a park each morning before breakfast. I began rewriting my young adult novel set in New Zealand.

But my life felt strange and sad. Though my husband was physically still with me, he was no longer able to share the life we'd built together. I was gradually becoming more independent, but I didn't much like it.

# 25

# Viaje Bien

The grief process is complicated and unique to each one of us. As I grieved the loss of the "old Chuck," emotions spun through me as if I were caught in a revolving door. Just when I thought I was done with the despair—or the anger, or the sadness—back it would come to knock me down again.

Nine months after Chuck's stroke, I thought I was coping pretty well. Then one dark morning in March, I boarded a Seattle Metro bus feeling terribly depressed. I walked down the mud-streaked aisle and slumped into a rear seat, hoping no one would sit next to me. The bus reeked of wet wool and mothballs. A noisy heater blasted hot air across my legs, and raindrops slid down the window. I stared blankly at the bus's overhead signs honoring the Metro Employee of the Year and the Metro Mechanic of the Year.

Next to them was a sign titled "Ride right" that explained how to be a good bus rider by not bothering others and having the correct change. Its grammar bothered me. The Spanish version was better: "Viaje bien." Ride *well*.

But I was not riding well that day. Not even close.

I knew where I was going and what I would do when I got there: I was scheduled to record a radio show at the library for the blind. But I felt completely without purpose, energy, or even a shred of understanding about why that might be important or why I was going through these familiar motions.

Chuck wasn't going to get better, and at that moment I wasn't sure I was either. I didn't understand what I was supposed to do in this brave new world. As his wife, I think I was supposed to take care of him. But apparently, I'd failed at that.

The bus turned away from the waterfront onto Yesler Way, bringing into view a succession of dreary storefronts. We passed an empty Japanese restaurant with grimy windows. I'd never eaten there and I never would. Two human-sized teddy bears sat propped at a table in a shop that sold only chocolates. A chain-link fence secured with padlocks surrounded a boarded-up building. Who knew what that used to be? A brick alleyway meandered south toward the stadiums where a man poked around a Dumpster overflowing with garbage.

For the first fourteen years that Chuck and I lived in Washington, we rode the 8:45 a.m. ferry to Seattle every Wednesday. We bought egg sandwiches on the ferry and ate them while we penciled in the *New York Times* crossword puzzle. In Seattle, we hiked up the hill to the public library where Chuck would spend his day doing research in the genealogy department. I would continue on to the Washington Talking Book & Braille Library to record mystery stories for their radio station. When we were finished, Chuck and I often met up for a movie and dinner before returning home.

That morning as I headed off to record another radio show, I wondered why I bothered. I never got feedback, so I didn't even know if anyone listened to my program. And if they did, I didn't know if they liked it or not. Over the years, I'd recorded dozens, maybe hundreds of mystery stories. But did anyone really care? Did I?

I don't know why on that particular day I was so plagued by the meaninglessness I saw in everything. After Chuck's stroke and dementia diagnosis, I took a break from my radio reading. I'd resumed because friends advised me to "keep doing it for continuity's sake." Right then, that didn't seem like much of a rationale.

The bus hissed to a stop four blocks from the library. I disembarked and began walking through the rain. I had worn the wrong coat—mine was too thin for the cold wind—and I'd forgotten my umbrella. My lethargy quickly slid into despondency. I longed to be home, though I felt fearful and skittish when I was there. Whether I was alone in my rural house or with people in the city, it didn't seem to make any difference. Everything was a big mess, and I didn't know what to do.

I lifted my hood and walked on. A block from the library I passed a bus shelter. As I walked by, avoiding puddles on the sidewalk, I glanced inside. Two African American men in hoodies squatted against the back wall. They looked cold in their thin sweatshirts and tattered sneakers. It was obvious they weren't waiting for a bus. They were trying to keep out of the rain. The taller of the two men was looking at me. His brown eyes caught mine and he said softly, "God bless you, ma'am."

His words almost stopped me in my tracks. I wish they had. I wish I'd had the presence of mind to stop and thank that man for his blessing, which I so needed.

Instead, I kept walking, but with questions flooding my mind. *Who has a roof over her head? Who has a refrigerator full of food? Who has dry clothes in her closet? Who has a bank account filled with abundant funds? Who has greater faith?*

*Who is riding well?*

# 26

# The Public Is *Not* Allowed
# in Linen Closets

Chuck continued to be brave even while living in the clamp of dementia. He got up every morning, did the best he could, and didn't complain. I wanted to be brave like him. But in my life as a caregiver, my way of being brave had to be different.

For me, being brave began with waking each morning to an empty space next to me in bed and getting up without rupturing my heart. My brand of bravery meant walking through the front door of St. Thomas Health & Rehabilitation Center every afternoon, unsure of what challenges were waiting for me. Being brave meant continuing to love my husband despite his alarming transition from the patient man I had married to a man who sometimes acted unreasonably or incomprehensibly.

As you can guess, things didn't always go smoothly. There were many days when I was not brave. I cried. I despaired. I wanted out. But I kept my feet moving. Being brave did not mean being unafraid. Being brave meant getting up each day in spite of being afraid. What choice did I have?

Each time I entered St. Thomas, I girded my introverted self for possible battle in defense of Chuck. And on some days, I did need to go to war: confronting someone (his aide, his hall nurse, Sharon) over a diaper badly in need of changing, an untreated urinary tract infection, a call light left on for an hour, or his weekly bath postponed because of inadequate staffing.

But I picked my battles carefully. I couldn't take a chance that some disgruntled employee might make Chuck pay for something I'd said or done. With very few exceptions, I trusted the aides and nurses at St. Thomas. But Chuck was one of many patients, and sometimes the staff didn't have the time or energy to give him the care that he—or any other patient—deserved. Fortunately, the peaceful days outnumbered the "go to war" days. But when I walked into the nursing home, I never knew which reality would be waiting.

On lucky days when he was alert and happy to see me, I could slip off my armor and enjoy my afternoon with him. I could take him out for a latte and a drive, proving that small pleasures still existed and life mattered enough to keep on living.

At the beginning of each visit we greeted one another with a hug, followed by my quick assessments. Was he wearing a clean shirt and dry pants? Pillows or spilled food on the floor? Hair and beard combed? Curtains opened? Lunch bib still on? Bed linens in need of changing? Laundry basket emptied? If these or any other tasks needed to be addressed, I usually did them myself. Why? Because waiting for an aide to respond to Chuck's call light subtracted valuable minutes from our time together outside the nursing home.

To get him ready to leave the facility, I changed his diaper in the bathroom (which involved transferring him from his wheelchair to the toilet and back), put on his shoes—and coat, hat, scarf, and gloves in cold months. Then I wheeled him out to my van and transferred him into the front seat.

Many times as I knelt on the hard linoleum floor in his bathroom, I was amazed to think that we had once been a young, vibrant couple who never could have imagined this scene. I felt like the wife in Arthur Miller's *Death of a Salesman*. Like Linda Loman, I wanted to say emphatically, "I don't say he's a great man....He's not the finest character that ever lived. But he's a human being, and a terrible thing is happening to him. So attention must be paid!"

But no one seemed to be paying attention. Sometimes it made me sad that no one could see what was happening to us. Then one day I thought, *God sees us. And maybe God's heart is breaking too.*

In April 2004, Chuck's birthday was approaching—his first since entering the nursing home. I said to him (cheerfully, I thought), "Your special day is coming up soon! Do you remember when your birthday is?"

"Yes. I do."

He wasn't going to make this easy for me. "When is it?"

"25 April 1934."

"Right! And do you know how old you're going to be on April 25th?"

"No. I do not."

"You're going to be seventy!"

No response.

People had been asking what they could do for Chuck, and this conversation gave me an idea. I contacted our friends and relatives and asked them to mail birthday cards to Chuck. On April 25, the kids and I took Chuck to an island restaurant to celebrate. After the waitress had cleared our lunch dishes, I told him he'd received a few cards.

I asked, "Would you like to open them now?"

"Okay," he said.

I brought out a stack of envelopes that spilled across the table in front of him. He had received exactly seventy cards. When he saw the pile, Chuck began to cry.

Chuck had now turned seventy, and I was fifty-seven—not old by today's standards. But I wondered when my caregiving would be over. And whenever I contemplated that, I felt guilty. Because what does the end of caregiving imply? Each day when I walked through the nursing home door, I thought, *Will it be one more day, one more month, one more year—ten more years?*

I discovered that it was easier if I thought: *Today I will do this. All I have to do is get through this day. I can do that.* I knew that one day would be the last day. And even though I'd been preparing for it for days and days and days, I doubted I would ever be prepared for it.

On one cognitively clear day shortly after his birthday, Chuck said, "I never want you to come here out of a sense of obligation."

A beautiful sentiment: I should only come to the nursing home because I wanted to be with him. And I'd love to tell you that I never walked into St. Thomas with any emotions other than devotion and love for my husband. But then I would be a liar. On most days, I dragged myself to the nursing home with dread and duty in my heart. I hated seeing him so diminished. I hated the things I had to do for him that he used to do for himself. I hated what our lives had become. I wanted an end to his suffering and to my caregiving. That is the truth.

An integral part of my caregiving routine became the spa bath or whirlpool. Early during his stay at St. Thomas, two aides gave Chuck the option of having this royal spa treatment, and he loved it. But those aides had quit and moved on. The ones who followed did not know how to operate the unwieldy apparatus, but Chuck refused to take the handheld shower that they had been trained to give him. He complained that he froze to death in the cold shower room.

After lengthy discussions with Sharon, the director of nursing, and the intervention of Dr. Farmer, I was trained to give Chuck spa baths. And I trained any aides who were willing to learn.

Chuck had been a daily shower-taker, and the nursing home offered residents one bath per week. Chuck's bath day was Saturday. But by bathing him myself on Tuesdays and Thursdays, I could ensure that he got three baths a week. Eventually, when none of the aides could or would operate the whirlpool, I gave Chuck all his baths. One of the challenges of the whirlpool was its tendency to leak—its door gaskets were ancient, and the whole machine seemed poorly engineered. More than once, I flooded the hallway outside the spa room.

In preparation for his spa bath, I would retrieve six bath towels, two bath sheets, and several washcloths and hand towels from the linen closet. Believe me, each one had its function in the hour-long process. While the spa's tank was filling with hot water (which took about twenty minutes), I would wheel the plastic shower chair to Chuck's room and undress him. Then I would push him, draped in bath sheets, down the hallway to the spa room. I reversed his chair into the whirlpool, shut the door, and let the water into the tub.

He would prompt me to start the jets by saying, "H.O." I never knew what this meant, unless it was an abbreviation for $H_2O$. One day he said, "Turn on the hurricane." After the bath, with bearded Chuck once again draped in bath sheets and a towel turban covering his wet hair, he resembled an elderly swami. As I wheeled him back to his room, people in the hallway sometimes asked him questions like, "Chuck, what is the meaning of life?"

Bathing my husband was one more activity I had never envisioned myself doing. On some days, as I scrubbed him with a washcloth and shampooed his hair and beard, it seemed terribly sad to see him so infirm and vulnerable. On the best days, washing him felt sacred. What could be more holy than to let hot water run over his cold shoulders and gently wash his body when he could no longer do it himself?

One afternoon I walked into the linen closet—a tiny room lined with wooden shelves—to retrieve my pile of towels for Chuck's spa bath. Sensing another's presence, I turned and saw a woman with short, stone-gray hair scowling at me.

"What are *you* doing in here?" she demanded. Without waiting for my answer, she said, "You're not allowed to be in here."

"I'm not?"

"We can't just let anyone wander in here off the street!"

Funny, I had never noticed people coming in off the street asking to go into the linen closet. I seemed to be the only one with an interest in that.

She told me she was the new Head of Laundry and that from now on, I must ask a staff person to assist me if I wanted anything from the closet. The next day a sign appeared on the door: "The Public Is *Not* Allowed in Linen Closets."

I complied for a few weeks, much to my annoyance and that of the aides who were now required to retrieve my towels. But not long after this closet confrontation, the head of maintenance came to me to apologize. He had fired the laundry lady for other issues.

"I'm sorry if she gave you a hard time. The way I figure it, you're doing us a favor."

I said that was how I figured it too.

So let's leave it at that. Some days visiting Chuck at the nursing home were horrible. Some were okay. Some were good. And a chosen few were blessed.

Chuck had hung *National Geographic* maps: one of the United States, the other of the world. Both maps bristled with color-coded tacks that marked spots where he or I—or he and I together—had spent at least one night of our lives. But the maps had grown tattered and dingy. And I didn't like encountering reminders of our past life every time I walked through the hall.

*Chuck pauses in his genealogical research long enough for me to photograph him in his home office on Bainbridge Island in 2002.*

But could I be so cavalier as to throw away his cartographic creations? And the next time I wheeled him into the hallway, would he notice his maps were gone and realize that his residency was over? Of course, it was, but I still couldn't find the courage to broach that subject with him. And maybe he preferred to keep that dream alive in the hopeless landscape of his life.

As the months passed, I began to emerge from my puddle of guilt, sorrow, and confusion. Still, memories of a healthy Chuck stalked me in every room. I needed to jettison Toxic House in order to begin my new life.

But I was stymied. I owned a house with four bedrooms, three bathrooms, a kitchen, laundry room, dining room, living room, and two offices—each room filled with possessions that prevented me from leaving.

And the hardest room to face was Chuck's office. Once we'd settled in Washington, Chuck devoted his energies to family history research. In addition to compiling both our family histories, he helped others all over the world with their genealogical queries. Chuck earned a reputation as a meticulously skilled researcher. He was sought after not only by individuals but also by companies looking for heirs to estates. Paying homage to his childhood's favorite radio show starring the fictional Mr. Keen, Chuck's business cards and stationery read: "Charles E. 'Chuck' Munat: Tracer of Lost Persons." His office was his genealogical research lab, and it represented a huge part of Chuck's vitality and self-worth.

Walking in there now made me physically ill. One day I was showing a friend through the house and when I started to enter Chuck's office, I halted abruptly at the door. She said I looked like a dog whose owner was trying to push her out into the rain. The room was filled with memories of a lively man happily immersed in his research, and now that man couldn't even type. He couldn't email his correspondents. He couldn't think clearly enough to create a family tree. He couldn't read or write. The man who had taught Shakespeare and Steinbeck could now barely read a newspaper headline or turn on his TV.

The few times I forced myself to enter his office, I could only stare forlornly at the chaos and leave. Once or twice I moved a box aside only to discover three more behind it. I couldn't face the task of cleaning out his office. So I resigned myself to staying at Toxic House.

That August marked the one-year anniversary of Chuck's readmission to St. Thomas. I went to our annual neighborhood Cornfield Potluck by myself because I couldn't have pushed Chuck's wheelchair over the rough terrain. I didn't tell him that I went to the party without him.

Nor did I tell him that St. Thomas had increased their rates, or that I had removed him as executor of my will, or that I sometimes made his favorite pizza for dinner and ate it myself, or that I dreamed of moving. I hated keeping secrets from him. But what was the point if they marginalized him even further?

Late one August evening, I sat on our second-story deck watching a movie on my laptop. I was fiddling with my gold wedding band when suddenly it flew off my finger, bounced on the glass table, rolled across the deck, and disappeared between two floorboards. I ripped off my headphones and hurried down the spiral staircase to the basement door. I flicked on the outside light and began to search. I knew the ring might not be visible in the dark, but I *had* to find it. I checked the entire concrete pad underneath the deck and poked around our stack of firewood. No luck. The ring could have rolled into the grass, which lay in darkness. Discouraged, I gave up and went to bed feeling strangely incomplete without my ring.

The next morning, my search was more thorough—but equally fruitless. I rechecked every square inch of the concrete pad, scoured the area around the woodpile, and moved into the grass, swishing the blades back and forth with my palms. After conducting the same search for days, I gave up and bought another gold wedding band.

That fall, a realtor joined Circle Babes, my women's support group. Though I still didn't know how to get rid of my house, I asked Ann if she might help me find a new place to live. In December 2004, she showed me several units at three different condo complexes. I had a strong preference for the first complex because of its wonderful water views—and its proximity to the ferry terminal and the island's retail core. But of the two units for sale there, the one I liked best was overpriced, and the other one needed remodeling.

In the second complex, the units were under construction and wouldn't be available for another year. The prices for units at the third complex were out of sight. Ann suggested we take a break and resume our search in January. My desire to move to a smaller home seemed more impossible than ever. But over the Christmas holidays, two things happened that inched me closer to my dream.

*Teddy and Chuck decorate one of Chuck's "Charlie Brown" Christmas trees
from the lot behind our house in Middletown.*

The first had to do with my missing wedding ring. Ever since our
first Christmas in Middletown, we had cut down our own Christmas
tree. Our property abutted a neighbor's field, and she gave us carte
blanche to take any tree we liked. I say "we," but it was Chuck who cut
our tree, and his taste ran to the Charlie Brown variety, much to our
children's chagrin. Year after year, Chuck would bring home an asym-
metrical hemlock or scrawny pine, and we'd all groan.

But once we'd hung the colored lights and bird ornaments on
it, our tree looked every bit as beautiful as a $50 white spruce from a
commercial lot. In Washington, Chuck cut trees from our small yard,
but after a few years no suitable ones were left—not even by Chuck's
standards. Undaunted, he began pruning deciduous tree branches to
decorate.

That December, I adopted Chuck's method and cut an arching branch from our California crepe myrtle. I set it up outside on the deck. On Christmas Eve morning, I was standing next to my "tree" with a lit strand of little white lights draped over my shoulder when the whole string of lights went out. After rummaging in our ornament box, I found a new fuse. But those things are tiny, and the fuse squirmed out of my fingers like a guppy, fell onto the deck, rolled between two floorboards, and disappeared. Déjà vu!

I walked down the spiral staircase, opened the basement door, and looked around the concrete pad. I spotted the green fuse lying right underneath where I'd dropped it. And next to the fuse was my gold wedding ring. I slid the ring onto my finger next to its replacement and have worn both ever since. Maybe it's a stretch, but the miraculous return of my wedding ring seemed as if Toxic House had given me its blessing to leave.

A second miracle occurred on December 26, the holiday called "Boxing Day" in Commonwealth nations. On that day, our family gathered for its own private boxing day when Charles, Isabel, Ben, Ted, Judith, our niece Maggi, Chuck, and I sorted through all the boxes and file cabinets in Chuck's office.

A local moving company provided cardboard boxes, and we filled thirty of them with Chuck's genealogical papers, computer disks, and family history books. I had made arrangements to donate everything to a library in Georgia that specialized in Scots Irish family histories like many that Chuck had researched. And I'd hired a trucking company to pick up the materials and transport them to Georgia.

Chuck had kept a personal file for each year of his life. While perusing these, our children discovered some mementos and keepsakes such as letters, photos, poems and stories they had written during their school years. Ted claimed Chuck's Chicago Taxi Driver ID card from 1956, the year he drove a cab while waiting to be drafted into the army. We had bins for papers we were throwing away and took turns hauling them to the recycling center.

Chuck, a genealogical packrat, sat in the middle of the room in his wheelchair overseeing the action. He'd always been a person who'd organized his life on paper, and he hated throwing anything away. But that afternoon I showed him a carbon copy of a letter he'd written and asked if he wanted to keep it. He glanced at the letter and said, "Ben showed me that already, and I said good-bye." Chuck had always been a realist, and some aspects of his personality hadn't changed.

Two weeks later, a moving truck arrived to pick up Chuck's genealogical lifework. The driver stacked the boxes on his hand truck and ran it in and out of our front door. Each time the hand truck passed over the doorsill, it made a loud whack that felt like a hammer to my heart—driving home the fact that Chuck's life as a venerated genealogist was over. The incremental losses during a long caregiving experience just keep on coming. When the truck pulled away from the curb outside our house, I burst into tears.

I telephoned an office furniture company and offered to give them Chuck's lateral file cabinets if they would come and cart them away. After they'd removed them, Chuck's office was empty. For the first time in fifteen years, I vacuumed it.

# 28

# Awe and Gratitude

After Boxing Day, I slowly but steadily plowed through the tasks necessary to dismantle our household. The gardeners hauled away Chuck's power tools and the basement bedroom furniture. I took donations to Goodwill, the public library, and my church's rummage sale. One morning with a heavy heart, I got out the duffel bag that Chuck had taken to New Zealand on all six of our trips. I laid it on our bed and packed up the remaining items in his closet: shirts with buttons, slacks with zippers, and shoes with laces—clothes he could no longer put on without assistance. His new wardrobe had become sweatpants, pullover shirts, and shoes with Velcro fasteners. I dropped the bag off at Goodwill that afternoon on my way to the nursing home.

My realtor Ann advised me to sell the big house "as is" because we knew it was beyond my current capabilities to orchestrate any home improvements. Luckily, before I put it on the market, my next-door neighbor decided to buy it as an investment.

I brought Chuck the papers he needed to sign as co-owner of our house. When I laid them on his tray table, I thought about how devastating this moment must be for him. It meant that we would never again live under the same roof. "I'm sorry if this makes you sad," I said, handing him the pen. "It must be very hard for you."

He scrawled his illegible signature on the papers. "No, it's not sad. It's not my house anymore." Well, what do you know? I'd been assuming he still wanted to live at home when apparently he'd accepted his reality, and it was me who hadn't.

The second piece of relocation fell into place when Ann helped me negotiate the purchase of the second-floor unit in the building near the ferry terminal that I'd loved from the beginning. Closing day was set for

May 20, 2005, and moving day would take place the following Friday, the start of the Memorial Day weekend.

I awoke on May 27, 2005, with the realization that I had just spent my last night at Toxic House, and I felt deep gratitude. Not so much because my tenancy was over, but because this place had served as our gracious home for sixteen years. While waiting for the moving truck, I sat on the front doorstep, sunshine dappling my lap, and I remembered some of the times that Chuck and I had shared here.

Three months after we'd moved in, we held our Twentieth Anniversary Party in the living and dining rooms. Everyone helped us celebrate: our kids, our new neighbors, Chuck's cousins from Seattle, and James Travers and his five-year-old son Spencer from New Zealand! Isabel preserved some funny family moments with her video camera. Spencer, whose presence was a big surprise, said, "Grandma and Grandpa Munat, do you know what your anniversary gift is? Me!"

I recalled the Christmas when our three-year-old granddaughter Alex disappeared behind a wall of presents until we heard her small voice saying, "I think I've got enough!" And Sharky, clutching my finger when he was learning to walk in the kitchen. I remembered the times after long visits to New Zealand, trips to Puerto Vallarta, and car treks around the West—and how wonderful it felt to walk through that big front door and know we were home. I thought of summer mornings reading to Chuck on the deck while hummingbirds vaulted into the sky and emitted threatening chitters on their downward arcs.

The memories kept coming. Chuck and I glued to the living room TV on the morning of September 11, 2001. Alex and Sharky splashing in the wading pool in our shady front yard. Spirited family games of Pictionary in the dining room, where once the pencil of a frustrated artist flew across the table. The laundry room's awful lime-green and apricot cabinets. "Make Your Own Pizza Nights" with toppings in bowls on the kitchen counter, including Chuck's favorites: ham and pineapple chunks sprinkled with cinnamon. Climbing into the Japanese soaking tub to relieve the chill of winter nights. And I remembered how Chuck and I hugged and cried on the deck when Barbara Travers's funeral was taking place in Wellington, New Zealand. She had died of cancer, and her children—Spencer (13), Elliot (11), and Brittany (8)—were the same ages Charles, Isabel, and Ben had been when their mother died, also at age thirty-seven.

This house had seen us through many joys and sorrows over the sixteen years we'd lived in it. Perhaps it was a blessing that I found it so easy to leave.

Two young men in royal blue T-shirts moved my pared-down possessions into the new condo, and when they finished, all I had to offer them were Cokes and coffee cake. That seemed an inadequate reward for the huge favor of ushering me into my new life. But of course, many others had helped with that—my amazing children and my loyal friends. I could never have accomplished it by myself.

Alone in my new home, I walked around flicking light switches and peering out the windows at my new views. Filled with awe and gratitude that I had accomplished what once seemed impossible, I remembered that it was Chuck who had taught me never to give up on my dreams.

Even after darkness fell, it was warm enough to sit outside on my small deck. The velvet air caressed my skin as I watched the ferries come and go while the lights of downtown Seattle glimmered across the water. I felt like I'd never have to be alone again. My condo had already become a source of serenity and comfort. Now I could concentrate on becoming my own best friend, to treat myself with compassion and without judgment, which would allow me to be a kinder caregiver to Chuck. I whispered, "I think I can do this now."

That night I got into bed and leaned against the headboard Chuck had made in Middletown using cedar boards left over from building bookshelves. Tomorrow I would bring Chuck here. I would make him cinnamon toast and pour him a glass of his favorite nonalcoholic beer. I imagined him sitting by the window in his wheelchair, trying to count shorebirds in the harbor. As he and I passed through this transition—euphoric for me, indifferent for him—we still wore our shrouds of sadness. But when I poked around my chest for my pocket of dread, I realized it was gone. A terrible thing had happened to us, yet at this moment I was able to acknowledge the possibility that more happiness could come. It had taken me two years to arrive at this point.

*I brought Chuck to see my new condo in the spring of 2005.*

# 29

# C'mon, Papa,
# You Can Do It!

Gone were the four-day Thanksgiving and Christmas parties that Chuck and I used to host for our family at the big house, but I hoped the first Christmas at my condo would provide some new stories and moments of happiness. Ted and his three-year-old son Sharky were the first to arrive on Christmas morning 2005.

In the days after Chuck's stroke, Lillie and Sharky had extended their visit to our house so I would have company after my day at the hospital. Each evening as soon as I walked in the door, little Sharky would appear and grab my index finger. Time to practice walking! Using me as a fulcrum, he would walk in circles around the kitchen, whooping his pleasure each time he completed a circuit, eventually collapsing into my arms in giggles. Having a toddler at home helped me relax, and I could ask Lillie medical questions.

When Sharky was two years old, Ted and Lillie divorced, agreeing to share custody of their son. In the following months, both parents became concerned about changes in Sharky's happy temperament. His new behavior was hard to explain. Unfriendly? Dissociative? While not overtly hostile, Sharky emanated the strong impression he wanted nothing to do with any of us. At family gatherings he would march grimly past us, glaring at the floor. If someone greeted him, or even *looked* at him, he would jerk his head and yell, "No!"

He had little interest in toys, crayons, blocks, and books. At the Waterfront Park playground, he ignored the slides and swings, instead focusing his attention on the wood chips, which he let fall through his fingers over and over again. He seemed to be retreating into a narrow world of his own creation, a world that did not include grandparents, uncles, aunts, cousins, and barely his mother and father.

Ted had custody of Sharky from Friday to Sunday. But Ted lived in Olympia—sixty miles south of Seattle where Sharky and Lillie lived. After negotiating awful Friday afternoon traffic on Interstate-5, Ted would bring Sharky to my apartment for the weekend instead of returning to Olympia.

During many of those nights at my condo, Sharky would refuse to sleep, throwing howling tantrums when Ted tried to put him to bed. In desperation, Ted would strap Sharky into his car seat and drive around the island until the little boy fell asleep. When Ted's car was nearing my apartment, he would phone me to come downstairs and open the stairwell door. Our hopes would rise when Sharky stayed asleep in Ted's arms during the walk up the stairs. But when Ted laid his son on the bed, the wailing resumed. On some nights, sleep never came for father or son, and the next day both were groggy and irritable.

Sharky would not interact with me, and he didn't acknowledge Chuck when I brought him back to the condo. And he never said our names. If he noticed we were looking at him, he would shout, "No!" Other than these cries of dismay, he was almost nonverbal. This painful situation had become the norm. (The following year, Ted and Lillie requested that Seattle school district personnel evaluate Sharky, and their testing led to a diagnosis of autism.)

When Ted and Sharky arrived on Christmas morning, Ted and I began preparing dinner in the kitchen while Sharky marched into the living room without a glance at me. I had no expectations of any exchanges between Sharky and Chuck either. Suddenly the electric power went out! I was worried about roasting the turkey, but when I called the electric company they promised that power would be restored quickly. Using the oven was crucial, but we wouldn't need to turn it on for a few hours.

Around midday I left to pick up Chuck at St. Thomas. I helped him into his Santa suit before driving him to my place. In the condo's carport, I transferred him from the minivan to his wheelchair. While whistling "Once in Royal David's City," I pushed him over to the front door and wondered why the lobby was dark. Then it came to me: the power was still out! This meant that the elevator that had always carried Chuck's wheelchair to the second floor was out of commission.

I wheeled Chuck to the stairwell door and left him there in the sun while I ran upstairs to confer with Ted. Besides the dead elevator, the only way up was this staircase—eight steps to the first landing, a 180-degree turn, and eight more steps to the top. Chuck hadn't walked up a flight of stairs in two and a half years.

Ted and I reasoned that if we grasped Chuck's arms and held him upright, he might be able to move his legs and ascend the stairs. Maybe. We would almost have to carry him, and he was over six feet tall and weighed 190 pounds. From the second-floor walkway outside my apartment door, Ted and I leaned over and called down to Chuck, asking him what he thought of our idea. Chuck said it was a wonderful plan—that he was perfectly capable of walking up a flight of stairs. But then, Chuck often had a higher opinion of his physical abilities than the rest of the world. However, we had no options.

I grabbed a white plastic chair from my deck and positioned it on the top landing where Chuck could collapse into it, assuming he made it that far and didn't crumple on the stairs first. At the bottom of the stairs I found a wooden shim to prop open the door.

We assumed that Sharky would stay in the apartment while we tackled this task, but he followed us out the door and down the stairs. I had some concern that he might get underfoot or inhibit our efforts in ways I hadn't yet envisioned. Ted later admitted to similar misgivings.

Standing behind Ted, Sharky peeked out the stairwell door. He saw not only his white-bearded grandfather sitting in a wheelchair, but Sharky also took in the red and white Santa suit, the black boots, the red floppy hat—the whole deal.

Looking stunned, Sharky began chirping, "Papa is Santa Claus! Papa is Santa Claus!" He repeated this phrase over and over, each time emphasizing "Papa" a little more joyously and incredulously. Ted and I were incredulous too. Before that moment, neither of us knew that Sharky had a name for his grandfather.

When Sharky had finished exclaiming, I pushed Chuck's wheelchair into the stairwell, and Ted and I assumed our positions on either side of him. Sharky scampered around the three of us and up the stairs to the first landing where he turned and peered down. On the count of three, Ted and I hoisted Chuck out of his wheelchair, and he gamely began to mount the stairs. Ted and I gripped his arms with intense concentration—knowing that one slip could result in a disastrous fall for all three of us. As I shoved my thigh into Chuck's butt to propel him up to the next step, I questioned the wisdom of our decision. Despite Chuck's optimism about climbing the stairs, his legs were shaky and he began to wheeze.

Then a small voice came from the landing. "You can do it! You can do it! C'mon, Papa, you can do it!"

*Chuck and Sharky relaxing after Papa climbed the stairs on Christmas Day.*

Glancing up, I saw Sharky's animated face and his arms raised over his head, his fists balled like a cheerleader's. Then he lowered his arms and with palms out, he cautioned, "Slow down, slow down. Take it easy." Lifting his arms over his head again, he continued cheering, "You can do it!"

By the time we reached the first landing, Ted and I were finding it difficult to remain upright—not only because of Chuck's weight balanced between us—but also because we were giddy and giggling over Sharky's antics.

The little guy scooted up the second set of stairs and resumed his "You can do it!" chant to Papa from the top landing. When at last Chuck mounted the final step, weary with effort, he did indeed collapse into the waiting chair. Jumping with glee, Sharky put his arms around his grandfather and kissed Chuck's reddened cheek.

"Good job, buddy. You did it! Good job, Papa!"

And Papa smiled.

# 30

## Going Solo

My transition to the life of a single person felt unnatural and awkward. I always found it fun to travel or go out to dinner with Chuck. But it was *not* fun for me to travel or go out to dinner by myself. So I stayed home a lot. Once half of a duo, I was now going solo. But slowly I began to understand that my family and friends were reaching out to help me adjust. All I needed to do was to say Yes.

One night in March 2006, Charles, Isabel, and Ted asked me to meet them in Seattle—where all three now lived—for a 6:30 dinner at Shanghai Garden. My first instinct was to make an excuse about why I couldn't go. At the end of an afternoon with Chuck, the only thing I wanted to do was go to my condo and settle into my nest. But the kids had planned this gathering for my sake, so I agreed to meet them.

This excursion required that I ride the ferry to Seattle and walk about a mile to the International District. When I disembarked the ferry, I headed down the pedestrian walkway, which passes underneath the elevated Alaskan Way Viaduct and ends at First Avenue. At 6:00 p.m., a cold drizzle was falling in the near-darkness, and I began to wish I'd never come. I envisioned myself in my cozy chair by the window where I could gaze at Seattle in the distance—far preferable to actually *being* in Seattle.

When I reached the intersection of First and Marion, I saw a tantalizing vision: a brightly lit #56 bus waiting in the Ride Free Zone. Both front and rear doors stood open and seemed to beckon me to come on in, take a load off, and get warm. I figured I could ride south on First Avenue and hop off near the restaurant. I boarded the bus and sat down, feeling a little uneasy that I hadn't asked the driver how far south the bus went. No matter. I would just watch the street signs.

Wherever I got off had to be closer to the restaurant than where I'd gotten on, right?

The doors closed with a whoosh, and we pulled away from the curb. After traveling half a block south on First Avenue, the bus made a right turn onto the on-ramp of the Alaskan Way Viaduct. Before you could say "Mu Shu Shrimp," we were traveling south on the elevated freeway until downtown Seattle was just a watery smudge in the bus's rear window. I tried to visualize where the elevated viaduct would return to street level. I could get off there and board a northbound bus back downtown.

But just then, the #56 hung a sharp right onto the West Seattle Freeway and shifted into higher gear, heading due west. I turned in my seat to see the last vestiges of the Alaskan Way Viaduct disappearing into the mist—as were my chances of meeting my family for Chinese at 6:30.

Twenty minutes later, the bus made its first stop. Fortunately I had enough change to pay my fare. After I stepped off the bus, I surveyed the unfamiliar surroundings. I'd only been in West Seattle once, and it was definitely not at this intersection whose streets were lined with fast-food restaurants and convenience stores. I crossed the street to check the bus schedule. One was leaving soon for downtown, but I'd just used up all my change. So I walked through the drizzle to a 7-11, bought a roll of Mentos, got some change, and came back just in time to see the downtown-bound #56 disappearing around the corner. Back at the bus shelter, the schedule showed the next bus leaving at 7:00. It was now 6:25.

I phoned Isabel. She was sympathetic and offered to come get me, but I told her that wouldn't be possible because I didn't know where I was.

I stood under the roof of the bus shelter, scolding myself that if the old Chuck had been with me we never would have gotten into this mess—or if we had, being lost would have been fun instead of like sticking a pencil in my eye. My phone rang. This time it was Charles.

"Isabel says you're in West Seattle. What are you doing there?"

"I don't know."

"Where in West Seattle are you?"

"I don't know."

"Okay. I'll come and get you."

"You won't be able to find me. I'll just wait for the next bus."

"You don't have to do that. I'll find you."

"How?"

"Don't worry."

"I'm standing under a Taco Time sign."

"Good. Stay there."

Minutes later, his car pulled up to the curb.

I asked, "How did you do that?"

"I drove the way I thought the bus would go."

Dinner with my children was lots of fun, and the green barley noodles they recommended tasted delicious. Since none of them trusted me to take another bus, Isabel drove me to the ferry terminal after dinner.

Back home in my nest, I sat in my cozy chair by the window and looked at the lights of Seattle, the place where I'd just had an adventure I wouldn't have had if I'd said no. After reminding myself that *Yes* could be my new mantra, I went to bed and slept very well.

# 31

# Double Tall Nothings

As Chuck's nursing home advocate, I occasionally had to confront someone on the staff—and I hated those times. On other occasions, I had to battle Chuck himself when his confusion, frustration, and antipathy for his life—and possibly his jealousy of my freedom, when he had so little—caused him to become petulant and uncommunicative. I hated those times even more.

One cold afternoon in April 2007, I drove a sullen Chuck to an out-of-the-way café we rarely visited. I bought him a double tall nothing—a latte with two shots of decaf espresso and skim milk—spiked with two envelopes of artificial sweetener and sprinkled with cinnamon. Then I drove to a tiny parking lot next to a pier on the west side of the island. I thought he might like the change of scenery. He was wearing his Greek fisherman's cap and navy blue parka. I handed him his latte.

After holding the cardboard cup for about two seconds, his hand jerked (the medical term for this kind of spasm is "myoclonus"), and he dropped the latte. The cup's plastic lid popped off and twelve ounces of milky coffee formed a Rorschach blot on the van's carpet.

I snapped, "That was money well spent," and reached into the backseat for a roll of paper towels. He stared stonily at the dashboard and said, "I want another one."

I took a few deep breaths, finished mopping the carpet, and drove two miles back to the café where I ordered another double tall nothing. The barista looked puzzled as she made the second drink, but I silently paid, got in the car, secured the latte in a cup holder, and drove back to the pier in a rain shower.

This time I made sure Chuck had a firm grip on the cup before I let go, and then I picked up our current book. "All right. We left off yesterday—"

"I want to sit outside."

I chuckled. "Honey, it's raining."

Louder: "I want to sit outside."

"I didn't bring your raincoat."

"I don't care."

"Or an umbrella."

"I want to sit outside!" His eyes shot daggers at me. "Why don't you listen to me! Why? Why? Why?" He pounded the dashboard with his hand. "I want to sit outside! You never listen!"

My heart boiling, I retrieved the wheelchair from the back of the van, unfolded it, put the foam cushion on the seat, and rolled it through the wet gravel to the passenger door. Chuck opened the door and swiveled so that his feet hung out, almost touching the ground. Grasping the back of his sweatpants with both hands, I transferred him over and down into the chair, feeling his weight in my forearms. The rain picked up.

"Where do you want to sit?" I asked him.

"Here."

He sat in his wheelchair beside the open van door and drank his latte, as stubborn as a barnacle on a rock. I rested inside with the windshield wipers on intermittent and the heater going. After a few minutes, he said quietly, "I want to get in now." Silently I transferred him to the passenger seat, folded up his wheelchair, and hefted it into the van.

Back in the driver's seat, I asked, "Would you like me to read to you now?"

"No."

"What do you want to do?"

"Go back."

I drove him to St. Thomas where I settled him in bed, reminding myself that his anger was not directed at me, but at the restrictions that had been placed on his life.

I could see that Chuck's cognitive function and physical dexterity were getting worse. He needed me more than ever, which probably made him feel excruciatingly dependent on the partner with whom he'd once shared a life of reciprocity. No wonder he'd told me more than once, "I'm unproductive! What's the point?"

My response was always, "Chuck, you're showing me and the children and everyone else how to lead a full and dignified life under these circumstances. What could be more productive than that?"

Saying those words made *me* feel better. But I don't think Chuck bought it for a minute. He'd always been a man of action whose passion was to help others. And now with the passing of each day, he was becoming more and more dependent on others to help him.

*Chuck, Ted, and Sharky at my condo.*

# 32

# This Is What Love Looks Like

Even after the Big Latte Spill, I continued to drive Chuck to our favorite bakery, about half a mile from St. Thomas. On days when he felt too weak to get out of the van, I would place his order for him—a double tall nothing and a whole-wheat roll, known locally as a pull-apart. Then I'd drive to our usual parking spot at the head of the bay where he would consume his treats while I read aloud to him. On days when he felt strong enough, I'd wheel him into the bakery, and we'd sit at one of the hand-painted wooden tables to enjoy our lattes and pull-aparts. Those were the good days, which were becoming rare as time passed.

On one of those good days in the fall of 2007, we were waiting in line next to a glass case filled with sweet-smelling cinnamon rolls when I noticed two beautiful teenage girls staring at us.

I couldn't decipher their expressions. Were they regarding us with sympathy or derision or pity? Or were they simply looking at us with no emotion or judgment at all? Did they notice that Chuck and I wore matching wedding rings, or did they think I was a paid caregiver? Did they even know what a caregiver was?

There was Chuck with his ponytail and scraggly beard, wearing his gray fisherman's cap and saliva-stained parka. The rest of his fashion statement included gray sweatpants, white compression stockings, and Dr. Scholl's sturdy shoes with Velcro fasteners. In my faded jeans, broken-zippered parka, and scuffed sneakers, I must have looked like I was recovering from the flu.

As we waited in line, I thought about my sister Susie's friend—the man who was killed when he rode his bicycle into a truck in New York.

I remembered how I had envied his wife because I thought she had emotional resolution—and I didn't.

But now after four years of caregiving, I wondered if maybe *I* was the lucky one. Yes, each time I walked into St. Thomas Health & Rehab, I faced the uncertainties of Lewy body dementia with its wild fluctuations. But I still had my guy. Was he diminished? Of course he was. But I could still greet him with a hug, tell him news of the family, take him for a drive, read him a book, put him in his Santa suit and bring him home for Christmas. And love him with all my heart.

I wished I could tell those fresh-faced girls, and anyone else willing to listen, "Please look carefully. Because contrary to all appearances, *this* is what love looks like."

*Enjoying lattes with our houseguest Betty at our favorite island bakery.*
*In the fall of 1968, Betty and I roomed together when we were*
*practice teaching on the South Side of Chicago.*

# EARLY-STAGE DEMENTIA
## 2000–2003

# 33

# Dad Doesn't Like
# the Year 2000

Below is an excerpt from *Us & Our World*, Chuck's family newsletter in which he refers to himself as "Dad Munat."

**DAD DOESN'T LIKE THE YEAR 2000**
*by Chuck Munat – Sept. 2000*

Seattle, WA, USA, 25 Sep—*Dad Munat doesn't like the year 2000. He wants to go back to 1999. "Too much bad news for me in this year," Dad tells U&OW. His bad news began on Friday, 12 May. That's the day he found out he had had a heart attack.... Dad's next bad news came in early July. A biopsy revealed Dad had cancer in his prostate gland ... In mid-July Dad got sick with coughing and fever. The doctor on duty at his clinic on a Saturday morning said Dad was seriously ill with a urinary tract infection ... The Sunday doctor had chest x-rays taken that showed Dad also had pneumonia. After ten days of antibiotics, Dad's urinary tract infection and pneumonia were declared cured. Dad wondered how he could be cured when he still had to run to the toilet every half hour or so and was still coughing and wheezing ... Meanwhile, Dad decided to have the prostate removed ... Surgery was set for 25 Sep at Bennett Memorial Hospital in Seattle. On 30 Aug Dad went to see Dr. Patel for a pre-op physical.*

*On 19 Sept. Dr. Patel told Dad he'd passed the treadmill test and was fit for surgery, but the doctor used the occasion to drop a third bombshell—Dad has diabetes. So in the space of a little over four months, Dad had been diagnosed with three deadly maladies—heart disease, cancer, and diabetes.*

*Come October 16 and Dad was feeling a lot better. His coughing and wheezing are about gone. His cancer had not spread. He is gradually regaining his strength. But it will take a while longer before his plumbing is back to normal, and he has a lot to learn about diabetes.*

# 34

# What It's Like
# Inside My Brain

After sixty-six years with no major health problems, Chuck developed more than his share of illnesses in Y2K. But at the end of that year, I informed him that his heart attack, diabetes, and prostate cancer had all been addressed and resolved. As far as I was concerned, his physical problems were over and he needed to get back to normal!

But I did not share my more troubling thoughts about his behavior. I could see that my fiercely independent husband was becoming more and more reliant on me. He wanted to come along when I ran errands, met a friend for coffee, or flew to Houston to visit my sister Barbie. Once garrulous, Chuck now seemed withdrawn in social situations, staring at the tablecloth instead of conversing with our guests. My usually cheerful husband showed signs of depression.

And if I were honest with myself, Chuck's physical abilities were changing too. A few years earlier, he could smack a baseball a mile and cruise around a tennis court. But now his strength had waned and his stride had become a shuffle.

Even more worrisome, he sometimes stumbled and fell on his afternoon walk, returning home with a bloody forehead or a sprained ankle. He developed something akin to restless leg syndrome, which made it hard for him to fall asleep. This disrupted his circadian rhythm, changing the order of his days. Shortly after we went to bed, he would get back up and watch TV or do genealogy until very late. Then, predictably, he'd sleep until midmorning. His fatigue often sent him back to bed for daytime naps.

I was baffled as I watched my sixty-six-year-old husband transform into an old man before my eyes. I concluded that he was letting his "three deadly maladies" define him, and his uncharacteristic defeatism worried me.

Other inexplicable things happened.

On a family drive to Olympic National Park, we pulled into a campground for our usual rest stop. When Chuck stepped out of the car, he laughed because he'd forgotten to put on his shoes. Later, when we walked in the meadows at Hurricane Ridge, Ted and our AFS Barbadian son David held Chuck's arms while he gingerly made his way down the rocky trail in his slippers.

*Shortly before his stroke, Chuck and I had dinner at the home of our good friends Doug and Pipper.*

When our granddaughter Alex had afternoon gymnastics or swimming lessons, Chuck and I often drove the twenty-five miles to Isabel's house. Chuck loved back roads, so one day I plotted a new route that avoided the major highways. I handed Chuck the map and asked him to cue me as I drove. He stared at the map for a few seconds and handed it back. "I don't think I can do that."

During our 2002 stay in Wellington, Chuck and I toured the Museum of New Zealand Te Papa Tongarewa with five others—including James and his twelve-year-old daughter Brittany. We split up to look at the exhibits and agreed to meet at noon in the cafeteria. Six of us assembled at the restaurant at noon, but Chuck was a no-show. We sent Brittany to search, but she couldn't find him. At 1:00 p.m., Chuck wandered into the cafeteria with no explanation about where he'd been.

I was either unable or unwilling to link all these incidents to a single problem. Instead, I blamed Chuck. I suggested we try marriage therapy, but after a few sessions, Chuck said, "I've got enough to work on for the rest of my life!" He looked so confused and sad that I felt sorry for him. I gained some insights by expressing my feelings to a professional counselor, but when she took my side during our joint sessions, I realized she wouldn't be able to help us find a compromise. So we stopped going.

Chuck gave me an obvious clue about his condition on the day Sharky was born, but once again I missed it. On June 30, 2002, Chuck and I stayed in a hotel in Olympia so we could be present at Lillie's Caesarean section, scheduled for 7:00 a.m. the next day. Chuck didn't sleep all night and was exhausted in the morning. So I drove to the hospital alone to attend Sharky's birth. Around 11:00, Chuck phoned and asked me to pick him up. I did, and we had a celebratory gathering in Lillie's hospital room. Then Chuck asked me to drive him back to the hotel so he could take a nap.

Tired of all the back-and-forth trips, I said, "Why don't you drive yourself?"

He looked at me as if I'd asked him to pilot the Space Shuttle. "I don't know where the hotel is."

I drew him a map, showing the right turn at the bottom of the hospital driveway, the straight shot into Olympia, and the right turn onto our hotel's street. I walked him outside because he couldn't remember where the car was parked. Clutching the map, the former Chicago cab driver hesitantly climbed behind the wheel. He said, "You may never see me again."

I thought he was kidding. "C'mon, it's not rocket science!"

As he put the van into gear, he glanced at me and muttered, "You don't know what it's like inside my brain." I didn't ask him to explain what he meant—maybe I didn't want to know. He made it back to the hotel by himself, and we never mentioned the incident again.

Instead, I continued to blame him for something that was not his fault. Rather than acknowledge the possibility that an illness might be causing his behavior, I concluded that the problem was his attitude. *There's nothing wrong with him,* I thought angrily. *He's just not trying!*

In other words, I was in full-scale denial. True, I didn't have the knowledge or vocabulary to define exactly what was happening to him or why, but something was definitely wrong. And I persistently refused to face it. In hindsight, I can see clearly that Chuck was in early-stage Lewy body dementia.

# Chuck's Bucket List

Long before the movie, *The Bucket List*, Chuck added two items to his list of things to do before he kicked the bucket. "Before I die," he told me, "I want to see the Grand Canyon and I want to go to Mariners spring training."

He and I had participated in Elderhostel programs in Washington, Baja California, and Chicago. So I browsed their catalog until I figured out an itinerary. "Arizona Landscapes" would transport us up the state's central plateau in eight days, from Phoenix (elevation: 1,124 feet) to Sedona (4,326 feet) to Flagstaff (6,910 feet) to the Grand Canyon's South Rim (c. 7,000 feet). Following that we would attend "Seattle Mariners Spring Training" in metropolitan Phoenix.

Prior to this trip, Chuck's dependency on me had increased even more and his solo activities had decreased. He still drove his bronze-colored 1987 Toyota station wagon into town for errands and sometimes stopped for a latte, but he rarely drove off-island, as if crossing the bridge represented a foray into enemy territory. Chuck spent the rest of his time researching genealogical projects or watching news, movies, or sports on TV with me after dinner. He'd even stopped joining me on our Wednesday morning trips to Seattle. The reasons he gave for abandoning our long-standing practice? His morning fatigue, and "I've used up all the library's resources"—which didn't seem possible. So I was heartened by Chuck's interest in attending another Elderhostel.

In February 2003, after five days of riding a bus higher and higher across central Arizona, we arrived at the South Rim of the Grand Canyon on a freezing, wintry day. Fog enveloped the park, and there was no view of the canyon. Zero. The next morning it snowed several inches. Along with some fellow Elderhostelers, we trudged through deep snow to a restaurant at the canyon's edge. We ate our lunch peering into dense cloud hoping for a glimpse of rock, any rock. Nothing. Afterward we walked back to our room, fending off sleet that felt like bees stinging our cheeks.

Our last day at Grand Canyon National Park dawned darkly. The Elderhostel guides bused us to a nearby town to watch an IMAX movie about the Grand Canyon. We learned that the canyon's origins go back six million years, and that Native Americans had lived there since at least 1200 BCE. That was interesting, but movie views of the canyon didn't count for squat on Chuck's bucket list.

We returned to our room at the lodge and prepared for another gloomy afternoon. Someone knocked on our door. The optimistic program director informed us that a bus would be leaving soon to make a final attempt to view the canyon at Yavapai Point. We almost didn't go. But we relented and donned our inadequate coats and the mittens we'd bought in Flagstaff. Several of us made the trip to the lookout and got off the bus at the viewpoint. Though it had stopped snowing, all we could see was fog and cloud.

But then, miracle of miracles!

Suddenly the clouds lifted, the sun came out, and the view of views emerged below us: the one-mile deep, colorfully striated canyon in all its unimaginable glory. We stood gazing at the vista long after our frozen bodies insisted we return to the warm bus. But how can one leave such a vision? We turned to go only when clouds began to fill the chasm again. As we walked back to the bus, Chuck quoted e.e. cummings: "i thank You God for most this amazing day." It was a line from the poem we'd read at our wedding.

The following afternoon we checked into our hotel in Phoenix where it was seventy-five degrees and sunny. We spent the next five days basking in our beloved baseball lore—hearing lectures, relearning how to keep a scorecard, and watching movies about the "Negro Leagues" and the women who played professional baseball during and after World War II. Chuck and I reminisced about Teddy's Little League teams, which he and I had helped coach. We laughed about the time a little boy running to second base veered and ran all the way into right field to avoid being tagged!

On three consecutive afternoons, Chuck and I sat in the sun-warmed bleachers at Surprise Stadium and cheered for our Seattle Mariners, who did their best to grant Chuck's second wish. To the delight of their avid fan—a man who would soon be too ill to attend another Elderhostel, fly in an airplane, or live at home—the Mariners won all three games.

# VALEDICTIONS
## 2008–2009

# Hop on the Roller Coaster

Fluctuating cognition is a core feature of Lewy body dementia. (Though some individuals experience LBD symptoms differently or not at all.) Fluctuations refer to the way a person with LBD can be cognitively aware one moment and out of it the next.

I never got the hang of those cycles. They surprised me every time. When Chuck was up, I thought we'd be flying high forever. When he was low, I thought, *Mayday! Mayday! We're going down!* Some people compare this up-and-down phenomenon to riding a roller coaster. Here's how one of our roller-coaster rides played out during Chuck's fifth year at St. Thomas Health & Rehab.

*DOWN!*

On Friday, Chuck caught an intestinal bug that was going around the nursing home. By the time I arrived that afternoon, his stomach flu symptoms were so bad that his aide had to hose him down in the shower room—yes, the one he hated because it was freezing cold. I was glad she'd taken care of him, but it was awful seeing Chuck languishing in bed. He groaned with fever and made no response when I stroked his arm and asked him how he felt. After he ate a banana for dinner, he managed to mumble, "It's confusing because I don't know where I am. I keep thinking I'm at 225 … Street."

"225 Dakin Street?" I asked. "Where you lived when you were a child?"

"When I open my eyes, I'm looking at water."

"Like at the condo?"

No answer.

These sorts of exchanges continued for two days.

*UP!*

On Sunday morning when I arrived at St. Thomas, Chuck described a dream he'd had about our Swiss AFS student. "Daniel was riding a motorcycle and when he got to a building he parked his motorcycle and went into the building, opened a window, and shouted to another man who was outside on his motorcycle, but that man didn't hear him." It was the longest sentence he'd spoken since his stroke. He paused and looked at me. "I love you, darling." Even though "darling" was a term of endearment he rarely used, I was pleased to hear it.

I smiled. "You must be feeling better."

"Yes, and I have a plan. This morning I'm going to eat breakfast in bed, but I'll feed myself. Then I'll get dressed and get up for lunch. We'll wait and see how I feel at dinner."

I handed him a piece of toast from his breakfast tray, and while he ate it I reflected on how well he'd been able to organize his day—"executive functioning," I believe it's called. Most people with dementia can't do that.

*DOWN!*

Confident that Chuck had recovered, I came to St. Thomas on Monday afternoon. I expected him to be tired but just as capable as he'd been the day before when he planned his Sunday meals. Instead, I found him in the bathroom practically unconscious. Wearing yesterday's clothes and with his long hair uncombed, his eyes were shut and he was leaning against the arm rail of the raised toilet seat. His words were jumbled. When I tried to push him upright, he yelled so loudly that someone in the hall asked, "What's *that?*" I got an aide to transfer a near-comatose Chuck to his wheelchair. With his eyes half-closed, he pursed his lips and puffed as if he were blowing out candles. After a couple of hours, I couldn't stand it anymore. I alerted the staff that I was leaving and drove home.

Late that night, his nurse telephoned and suggested that Chuck be hospitalized.

"Is he sleeping?" I asked.

"Yes."

"Then what's the point of taking him to the hospital?"

"They could do some blood work and find out what's wrong."

"But he's very disoriented," I told her. "Riding in an ambulance and then being poked and prodded by people he doesn't know isn't in his best interests."

"I'm just giving you that option," she answered curtly.

"And I'm saying don't take him to the hospital. But would you please do a urinalysis? He could have a UTI."

"Dr. Farmer will have to order that. I'll call him in the morning."

When I arrived the next morning I learned that the night nurse had forgotten to write up the order, so I made a second request for a urinalysis. Two aides used a hydraulic lift to hoist a dehydrated Chuck out of bed and onto the toilet where he slumped against me for twenty minutes until he'd produced enough for the test. Then because St. Thomas didn't have a courier, I drove the sample to the lab.

That afternoon Dr. Farmer called to say that the results were inconclusive, but just to be safe, he'd ordered an antibiotic for Chuck. He agreed with me that a trip to the hospital wouldn't have been a good idea.

"I dread the next time he has to go to the hospital," I said.

"He won't have to," Dr. Farmer said. "We can treat him right where he is."

"Really?" I could feel the weight sliding from my shoulders.

The doctor said, "Our main goal now is to keep Chuck comfortable. Not his longevity. Are you with me?"

"Absolutely," I said. "And so is Chuck."

"We've got his signed 'Do Not Resuscitate' order and his advance directive saying he wants no artificial hydration or a feeding tube. It's all on file in our office."

"Yes. Those are his wishes."

That night I tried to get Chuck to sip some fluids through a straw, but the concept of sucking seemed foreign to him and nothing went down. He indicated he wanted some cut-up peaches, but when I held the spoon to his mouth he clenched his teeth. Failure to eat or drink could lead us to a very dark place. An aide put him into bed, and I was tiptoeing from the room when suddenly he woke up.

"You're not leaving, are you? I want you near me."

When I sat back down on his bed, he grimaced. Alarmed, I said, "What's wrong?"

He said, "You're sitting on my leg."

"Oh, sorry! Well, you said you wanted me near you." He smiled. Since he seemed to be tracking better, I asked, "Why did you say you didn't want me to leave? Are you feeling sad? Or lonely?"

He closed his eyes. "Yes. And I feel like I'm going someplace."

"Where?"

"One never knows."

He fell asleep.

I felt certain that Chuck was dying. I knew that dying people often feel like they're leaving or going someplace. And even though Chuck's current confusion could be illness-related, his cognition had sunk to new depths recently. I shared these thoughts with our kids in an email and also asked their opinions about restarting Chuck's diabetes medication. At Dr. Farmer's suggestion, Chuck had gone off this med a few months ago, but lately his blood sugar readings had been high.

Charles wrote: "I don't think we should try to choose Dad's demise for him by treating some things and not others. Medication to reduce suffering only, not to prolong life."

Isabel wrote: "Several years ago, Dad and I were talking about the fact that he was too tired to climb hills in Seattle. I said that if he climbed the hills it would make him stronger. He said he didn't have a lot of years left. I said he could live until he was eighty or ninety. He said his mother died at seventy-four. I always had the feeling that he had convinced himself that he was only going to live as long as his mother had. Dad turns seventy-four in twelve days."

Ben wrote: "As always, I will stand behind whatever you decide to do. I imagine that, unfortunately, things will only get harder from here on out."

Ted wrote: "My opinions are secondary in importance (by a long shot) to Dad's own wishes, which he still appears to be quite capable of expressing. It seems to me that Dad has been unblinkingly steadfast in his desire to let death come, regardless of the manner in which it occurs. As his death becomes more of an imminent event, and as the realities of how it might come about become clearer, he has remained ever brave and true to his goal. We all have goals and ambitions in life. At this point Dad's only real goal and ambition is to die with dignity and grace under his own terms. I can't help but believe that in supporting Dad to live out his ambitions, we can all gain strength from the courage of his convictions, and from that, gain strength to realize our own ambitions. I think Dad would like that."

I emailed Dr. Farmer that we would *not* be restarting the diabetes medication and included our children's remarks. He wrote back: "This is an amazing email which will stay in my files. I agree." With my permission, he put in an order for Hospice. I arranged to meet some Hospice staff at St. Thomas the following Friday.

*UP!*

After a restless night, I cancelled my plans to take the 8:45 a.m. ferry to my volunteer job at the library for the blind, and instead drove to St. Thomas. I found Chuck dressed and sitting in his wheelchair, eating a bowl of cornflakes. He looked surprised to see me. "What are you doing here?"

"Um ... I was worried about you. So I came over to see how you were doing."

"Why were you worried?"

"You haven't been feeling well lately. And you've been acting kind of strange."

"Isn't this Wednesday?" I nodded. "Aren't you going to Seattle today?"

"I was, but I thought you might need me."

"Oh. That's nice. But why don't you go ahead? I'll see you this afternoon."

I shook my head to clear my thoughts. "You really had me worried. So I asked some people from Hospice to come and talk to us."

He put down his spoon and looked at me, but I couldn't read his emotions.

I said, "If you're against the meeting, I'll cancel it."

Chuck held out his arms and I stepped into them, resting my cheek on his shoulder. "I gave you a jolt," he said, patting my back. "But it's okay to talk to Hospice."

On Friday, the Hospice nurse arrived early at St. Thomas to check Chuck's medical records in detail and talk to Sharon. Then the nurse and the Hospice social worker came into Chuck's room. First they thanked us for calling them. "You were right to do that," said the nurse. "But Chuck, after looking over your records and talking to Sharon, we agree that it's not time for you to enter Hospice."

The social worker explained that they were required to present information to Medicare indicating that a patient had a six-month life expectancy. "This isn't the case now. But don't hesitate to call us again because situations can change quickly."

After the women left, Chuck said, "Well, that's good, I guess."

I hugged him. "That you're not ready for Hospice? Yes, that's very, very good!"

I'd been riding my own roller coaster—thinking that Chuck was dying, then being told he wasn't dying. That was quite a turnaround for my brain. I needed to practice a new mantra: *Don't script it.*

On the way home I hummed a few bars of the *Hallelujah Chorus*, and then I reminded myself, "Time to hop back on the roller coaster."

# 37

# The Power of Love

Kate—the sister of our New Zealand son James—and her husband Pete were making plans for a North American trip and asked if they could visit us in September 2008. We had met Kate and Pete at James and Barbara's wedding, and they were an important part of our international family. Of course I said yes to their request and looked forward to hosting them at my condo.

On the Saturday they arrived, I walked over to the ferry terminal to greet them. They intended to spend Sunday and Monday touring Seattle, and then devote the last day of their visit to Chuck. We planned to take him out to lunch and for a drive.

On Monday Chuck was too disoriented to have a spa bath, and on Tuesday morning he was the worst I'd ever seen him—curled up in bed, seemingly not knowing who I was, maybe not even who *he* was. I was terribly disappointed. And although I understood the LBD roller coaster, I was scared that his condition might mean it was time for Hospice.

I came back home and broke the news to Kate and Pete. But they wanted to visit Chuck anyway. The three of us walked into Chuck's room around lunchtime. His aides had put him in his wheelchair, but Chuck was slumped over with his eyes closed and his mouth open. Seeing him like that, Kate and Pete turned around and walked back out, needing a moment to regroup. When they returned, Kate asked me if she could talk to Chuck. The earnestness in her brown eyes convinced me to say yes, though I doubted he would understand a word she said.

Wearing a flowered skirt and short-sleeved black blouse, Kate stood by Chuck's wheelchair and stroked his arm. She spent the next several minutes quietly talking to him in her lovely Kiwi accent. She told him about every member of her family, including James who, having lost Barbara to breast cancer eleven years ago, had found his new love Jenny. He'd quit his stressful job as a meteorologist and was the happiest he'd been in years.

Kate spoke about her mother Gladys, whom Chuck adored, and related stories people had told at Gladys's memorial service the previous spring. There was the story of the distressed young woman with two small children whom Gladys spotted in a bus station. Gladys walked over to this stranger and asked if she could help, and the young mother, whose face was bruised, broke down and admitted that she was fleeing her abusive husband. She wanted to go to her mother's home in Masterton, but that was far away and she had no money. Gladys took them home and fed them. She gave them $500 for travel expenses and sent them off. Over the next few years, envelopes arrived from Masterton containing small sums of money until the $500 Gladys thought she'd never see again was repaid. In her will, Gladys left the woman $1,000.

*Kate, Chuck, and I in his room at the nursing home.*

As Kate spoke, Chuck's eyes flickered, then opened, and he began to track her. Kate told of James's high school friend Reggie, a poor

Maori boy whose mother had died and whose father was in prison. Twice, Gladys had flown with Reggie to the Maori carving school in Rotorua for an interview. Subsequently, he'd received a two-year scholarship and is now considered one of New Zealand's master carvers. At this, Chuck's eyes brimmed with tears.

Wide-eyed now, Chuck looked at Kate and said quite clearly, "And how is Spencer?" referring to James's eldest child. And she told him that Spencer had a good job in Christchurch, and that next year he'd be getting married to a lovely woman called SoonMay.

So Kate talked Chuck back from the darkness. And she did it by the power of her love. It was pretty much like witnessing a miracle.

# 38

# Black Nativity

I rarely drove Chuck off the island. After his stroke, our only trips to Seattle were for appointments at the hospital. But after his Lewy body diagnosis, seeing medical specialists and having high-tech tests had become unnecessary. If Chuck needed medical attention that couldn't be provided by the nursing home staff, Dr. Farmer came to his bedside.

However, there was one off-island event that Chuck treasured, and I did my best to get him there every December.

Chuck had always loved gospel music, and he loved the poetry of Langston Hughes, an African American who led the 1920s Harlem Renaissance. A few years after we moved to Washington, we were delighted to learn that the Total Experience Gospel Choir, a mostly African American ensemble, would perform Langston Hughes's gospel song play, *Black Nativity*, at a Seattle theater. We attended *Black Nativity* that year and every year afterward, including the previous five years when I'd taken Chuck in his wheelchair.

But attending the 2007 performance had been a struggle. When I arrived at St. Thomas to pick him up, he was asleep in bed in his pajamas even though I'd left instructions for the staff to have him ready for the 11:30 ferry. Snow showers made driving in Seattle difficult. At the theater Chuck insisted on drinking a large cup of tea, and then twice had to use the handicapped restroom (whose toilet was ridiculously low with no grab bars). After the show he was confused about where we were eating dinner and became angry when I drove to the ferry terminal instead of a restaurant. And this year, he was even more physically and cognitively compromised.

As December 2008 approached, I was tempted not to remind Chuck about *Black Nativity*. I knew how tough it would be for me to get him there. But I reflected back on how much Chuck had loved the colorful costumes, the graceful dancing, and the powerful singing of Christmas carols in gospel style. It was the highlight of his year. And I didn't know how many years he had left. So in the end, I broke down and bought tickets.

On the day of the performance, I arrived at St. Thomas around 11:00. This time he was sitting in his wheelchair ready to go, but he said that he hadn't slept all night and was experiencing ear pain. The hall nurse gave him two ibuprofen tablets and sent us on our way. I asked the ferry ticket seller if I could park next to the restroom on the car deck. That was fortunate, because halfway to Seattle, Chuck needed a toilet. Suffice it to say, it was a nightmare getting him in and out of the ferry bathroom. But after that, the day improved.

Theater workers had made room for Chuck's wheelchair by removing two seats from the second row, giving him an unimpeded view of the stage. The show began as always with the Reverend Patrinell Wright singing the first verse of "Joy to the World" as an a cappella solo. At the end of the verse she called out, "Now *every*-body sing!" And the choir joined her in a full gospel chorus—with the band providing such an infectious, toe-tapping rhythm that we in the audience couldn't help but sing too.

When I glanced at Chuck, the absolute joy on his face told me that he had entered another world—one where nursing homes and wheelchairs did not exist.

*Black Nativity*'s musical numbers and choreography varied from year to year, but you could always count on hearing a few favorites. One of those was "This Little Light of Mine." I knew it was coming when Evelina, one of the original cast members, stepped down off the stage into the audience. Her black hair was gathered into a bun, and she wore a stole of bright African colors over her black robe. Her smile radiated into the farthest corners of the theater as she began to sing, "This little light of mine, I'm gonna let it shine!" Accompanied by the choir and the band, she sang and worked her way down the front row, shaking hands with her right hand while holding the microphone in her left. As the electronic piano, guitars, and drums pounded out the melody and the audience clapped, Evelina began the next verse: "All around the world, I'm gonna let it shine!"

And then she spotted Chuck.

Without missing a beat, her eyes widened as if she'd just come across an old friend she hadn't seen in years. She couldn't reach his hand, but she smiled at him and waved. I saw the happiness on his face and thanked God that I'd decided to bring him. It felt like being back on Chicago's South Side at one of those spirited Operation Breadbasket meetings.

After the show, I wanted to go backstage to thank that lovely woman, but Chuck was tired and anxious to leave.

On the way home, I said to him, "Evelina remembered you!"

"Yeah." He smiled again and a faraway look came into his eyes.

"I guess you must be a pretty memorable guy."

"Yep," he said. "Crazy white guy in a wheelchair."

That was his last *Black Nativity*.

# 39

# Now My Grandfather Is in a Wheelchair

Other than myself, the family member who spent the most time at St. Thomas was our granddaughter Alex. She would often stay with me when her father James and mother Isabel had to work weekends or "0-dark-thirty" shifts. Alex was too young to be left alone at my condo, so every day at 2:00, she would come to St. Thomas with me. She never uttered a word of complaint while I ministered to Chuck—giving him long spa baths or preparing him to leave the facility. She would sit in his recliner and read or sketch, humming softly and twirling a strand of her blond hair around her finger. On the days when we took Grandpa back to my place, she figured out something many adults never did: that I could use some help.

Alex became adept at opening doors, folding the wheelchair, and even stowing it in the back of the van. The wheelchair was too heavy and awkward for her small body, yet she learned to maneuver it, insisting, "It's my job!" Before she and I left the nursing home for the day, Alex would climb into Chuck's lap so she could give him a kiss and say, "I love you, Grandpa."

When Alex was ten, she and Isabel were thrilled to attend President Barack Obama's Inauguration in January 2009. Afterward, Alex wrote an article about her experience for her school newsletter. Chuck cried when I read it to him, I think because he realized that his granddaughter had inherited his sense of social justice—and his ability to write a compelling newspaper article.

*In 1963, my grandfather went to Martin Luther King Jr.'s 'I Have a Dream' speech in Washington, D.C. Now, forty-five years later, I stood in the same place and watched the first African American man be inaugurated as the President of the United States of America.*

*Going to the Inauguration was completely unexpected. We (my Mom and I) worked on Barack Obama's campaign, and I guess my mom decided that I should see what I helped to happen. I enjoyed working on the campaign, but making phone calls was somewhat awkward because every once in a while people would ask, 'How old are you?' I would answer honestly, 'Ten.' But nothing could measure up to the experience of being at the Inauguration.*

*Chuck and our granddaughter Alex.*

*We stood in line in below-freezing weather for over two hours; but, amazingly, everyone was so cheerful. They struck up conversations with complete strangers. When we finally got to our seats, we were in the center section, roughly*

*1,000 feet from the podium. We stood on our chairs and looked back at the crowds. It was unbelievable how many people were there. You could not see the green of the grass anywhere. It was an ocean of red, white, and blue; after all, most people had American flags ... flags waving as far as the eye could see. There were millions of people stretching all the way to the Lincoln Memorial where Martin Luther King gave his speech, a little over two miles.*

*When the inauguration was over, people were even more cheerful. History had been made.*

*Now my grandfather is in a wheelchair. He, along with Martin Luther King, could not experience the Inauguration of President Barack Obama. But I was there to see both of their dreams come true and I will remember it for the rest of my life.*

*President Barack Obama giving his inaugural address from the West Steps of the US Capitol in Washington, D.C., January 20, 2009.*

# 40

# Eighteen-Year-Old Converts

Chuck had a theory about eighteen-year-olds. He taught English literature to many of those zealous, idealistic teenagers, plus he experienced our own four children passing through that age. And of course Chuck himself had once been eighteen. His theory postulated that every eighteen-year-old becomes a convert to something.

After a childhood without formal religious training, Chuck became an eighteen-year-old convert to Roman Catholicism. In high school and college he dated an Irish Catholic woman and that relationship motivated him to take catechism classes and be baptized. But reserving room for skepticism, Chuck took the confirmation name of Thomas— as in *doubting* Thomas. But like everything Chuck did, he practiced his Catholicism with enthusiastic commitment. When his romance with the Catholic woman ended, Chuck continued to attend 7:00 a.m. mass every day. He and his wife Pat both attended Loyola University, and Chuck's first teaching job was at St. Ignatius, a Catholic boys' high school a mile west of the Loop. Chuck and Pat launched themselves wholeheartedly into the Catholic Family Movement, and their three children were all baptized and named for saints: Charles Francis, Isabel Anne, and Benedict Joseph.

But by then it was the 1960s, and everything came under the metaphorical microscope for dissection and analysis. Chuck and Pat sat down one Saturday night with a bottle of wine and discussed their religion. "Do you believe in original sin? What exactly is the Trinity? What does substitutionary atonement mean, anyway?" By the time the wine was gone, so was their commitment to worship as Catholics. The next morning they did not attend mass, and they never went to church again.

By the time I met him, Chuck said his religion was pantheism. Simply put, he approached God through nature, eschewing a personal God and institutional religion. He said he found God in mountains, oceans, birds, and flowers, "but in the ways of man I find him not." He became an ardent birder and nature photographer. Others who have been linked to pantheistic beliefs include Albert Einstein, Ralph Waldo Emerson, Henry David Thoreau, D. H. Lawrence, Lao Tzu, and Ansel Adams.

I'd been raised in the Episcopal tradition. My dad served as Senior Warden for two ministers; Mom taught Sunday school, attended healing prayer services, and weeded the churchyard. After my eighth-grade confirmation, I faithfully attended my church's high school youth group, and my eighteen-year-old conversion was simply to strengthen my existing faith. In college I became a member of the campus Canterbury Club, sang in the church choir, and often attended a pre-dinner evensong service. I even went to England and spent a summer working and studying at Coventry Cathedral.

But then 1968 rolled around—that turbulent year culminating in the election of Richard Nixon. And I got out my microscope and did something similar to what Chuck and Pat had done a few years earlier. A particular sticking point of faith for me was resurrection. When I asked myself if I believed that Jesus had died a brutal death on a cross and a few days later walked out of his burial tomb, my answer was a reluctant "No." And if I didn't believe in resurrection, I thought it would be hypocritical to remain a Christian. So I left the church. Over the next thirty-five years I tried to treat my neighbor as myself and do what I thought was God's will. But I did nothing intentional to develop my spiritual life.

Chuck's illness changed that. Shortly after his dementia diagnosis, I realized that not only was I unprepared for his death, I was unprepared for my death. I made a deliberate decision to find a faith community. Without spiritual support, I would not be able to walk the next part of my journey. Going it alone was no longer an option.

Some friends brought me to their church, aptly named "Grace." That first Sunday at Grace, I couldn't stop crying. I doubt the Gospel lesson that day was the parable of the prodigal son, but it felt like it. I guess I thought there would be some kind of hell to pay for my thirty-five-year absence. There was not. I experienced a warm welcome home, no questions asked. Reaching out for help from the people of Grace was another step of progress in taking care of myself.

A few years after that weepy morning, a ninety-year-old woman with macular degeneration asked me if I would drive her to church. As often happens when you think you're doing someone else a favor, you end up reaping much more than you give—as I was discovering about caregiving. Virginia became my wise friend. Over time, she counseled me about many things and always listened carefully to my tales of caregiving. She encouraged me to take one day a week off from visiting the nursing home until I finally succumbed to her reasoning. Then she began entreating me to take two days off.

Virginia and I often discussed our faith journeys while driving to and from Grace on Sunday mornings. One time she asked me, "Do you believe in resurrection?" By then my spiritual practice had contributed to the positive transformation of my life. I had accepted my role as a caregiver, and I loved Chuck dearly. I had moved to a new home and was building an independent life.

Yet my answer surprised both of us. "Yes, I do," I told her. "Because it happened to me."

At age ninety-four, Virginia developed health problems that required full-time care, and she moved into St. Thomas Health & Rehab where she and Chuck had some interaction. On Christmas Day 2008, I dressed him in his Santa suit and wheeled him into her room. Much to his delight, she raved about the suit and his authentic white beard. A few days before Virginia died, I visited her and asked how she was doing. On oxygen and barely able to see or hear, she pronounced in that lovely Louisville drawl of hers, "I'm just fine."

Virginia left instructions for her memorial service at Grace. By then, Chuck seldom left the nursing home because it required too much effort. But he was adamant about attending Virginia's service.

Accordingly, I wheeled him into the wide sanctuary. I had brought him to Grace for a few concerts and dinners, so the setting was familiar to him. About two hundred wooden chairs were arranged in a horse-shoe-shape around the altar, as usual. Behind the altar, tall windows allowed views of trees and sky. As we waited for the service to begin, I read him the instruction printed in the program about the taking of bread and wine during the service: *Please know that at Grace Church this common meal is for all who feel moved to receive. This sacrament is God's gift to all, and is not tied to membership, doctrine, or creed.*

When the time came, I asked Chuck if he wanted to be wheeled into the circle of communicants. To my surprise, he nodded. He looked beatific as he bowed his head and held out his palms to receive a small piece of bread from the priest. Then he crossed his arms over his chest to indicate he would not take the wine.

After the reception I drove him back to the nursing home and got him settled into bed. He was exhausted. If you're thinking he became a seventy-five-year-old convert to Episcopalianism, he did not. As far as I know, he remained a pantheist to the end.

That day at Grace turned out to be the last time Chuck left the nursing home. It was the only time I'd ever seen him take communion, and the only time we'd taken it together. I couldn't help but think that Virginia had something to do with that. Just the sort of special blessing and valediction she would have wished for us.

# *LETTING GO*
## *March–July 2009*

# 41

# The Ides of March

At a Circle Babes support group meeting in early 2009, I surprised myself by blurting out, "I am so tired! I don't know how much longer I can do this. And Chuck is tired too."

After almost six years of the daily nursing home routine, Chuck and I had grown closer in deeply spiritual ways. We didn't always need words to communicate. Our new intimacy was both unanticipated and undeniable. Although incremental losses surrounded us, we were not overcome by them.

During his time at St. Thomas, I had come to love the "new Chuck," who was simply a different manifestation of the "old Chuck." They were interwoven parts of the same man, and I loved the Chuck who sat before me in his wheelchair as much as the one who had stood beside me at the Connecticut waterfall the day we promised to be husband and wife "for as long as our love shall last." Well, it had lasted a good long time: forty-one years. Although our lives had become ensnarled in the tentacles of Lewy body dementia, even illness could not take away what we'd always had: an abiding love and respect for each other. And that kind of love does not come to an end.

When my caregiving saga began, I realized that one day we might be faced with the question, "What makes existence meaningful enough to keep on living?" That question came into clear focus one night at St. Thomas Health & Rehabilitation Center. It was March 15, 2009. Beware the Ides of March. (In his teaching days, Chuck would have added, "Act I, scene 2, the Soothsayer to Caesar.")

When I walked into his room that night, Chuck was lying in his bed staring at a blank television screen. He glanced at me and said, "I feel terrible."

For the past several weeks I'd adopted a new visiting schedule. Instead of arriving at 2:00 and leaving at 5:30, I'd been coming to the nursing home twice a day to feed him lunch and dinner. Chuck's manual dexterity had declined to the point where he had largely lost the ability to feed himself. He managed to eat the finger foods on his breakfast tray—toast and fruit and bacon.

But if I didn't show up, an aide would have to feed him lunch and dinner in the small dining room. The residents who ate in this room were severely disabled. Many lived in wheelchairs with seat backs angled backward so those poor souls—some of them quite young—would not fall onto the floor. In one corner of the ceiling, a fan blew continuously to rid the room of odors.

Chuck understood that if he had to eat meals in the small dining room instead of his private room, it would be a huge downward shift in the quality of his life. I had been delaying this step by showing up at mealtimes, but I wasn't sure how long I could keep up my twice-daily visits.

His extreme fatigue meant we could no longer leave the facility. He also had periods of unresponsiveness, like the day Kate and Pete visited. These episodes were often caused by urinary tract infections or other physical problems. But sometimes the culprit was overstimulation. The previous Thanksgiving at my condo, after spending three hours with too many people and too much noise, Chuck had shut down. His self-feeding at dinner had not been pretty, and soon afterward he slumped over the table in his gravy-stained bib, unable to respond to questions. I managed to transport him back to St. Thomas where an aide helped me put him into bed.

That night I wrote in my journal, "It is a sad and lonely feeling when he gets like that. It's like our partnership is just dribbling away, and I'm left holding the memories of what it was."

On the Ides of March when Chuck said he felt terrible, I asked him where his pain was. He waved away my question with his hand. "Not that kind of pain."

After six years of his aphasia, I was accustomed to filling in the blanks for him. "Do you mean you're sad? Or depressed? Or lonely?"

"All of the above."

At that moment two aides arrived. "Hi, Chuck, it's time to get up for dinner!" They proceeded to lower his head with the electric bed control. Flinging back his blanket, they removed his diaper, applied some zinc cream, put on a dry diaper and clean pair of sweatpants, raised him up, and with a "One, two, three," they hoisted my husband into a sitting position on the edge of the bed. While one aide retrieved Chuck's wheelchair and positioned it at a forty-five-degree angle to the bed, the other stood in front of him with her arms around his torso. Another "One, two, three," and Chuck was lifted up, spun around, and plopped into his chair, which was then pushed to the other side of the bed and positioned in front of the television. I rolled his tray table in front of him.

The aide asked loudly, "Do you want your TV on, Chuck?" He shook his head.

"Actually, *his* hearing's fine," I said. "I'm the one who's deaf."

She carried in Chuck's tray, removed the silver cover from the plate, and hurried off to help the next resident. Dinner was a roast beef sandwich on white bread, potato chips, a small dish of canned pears, a carton of milk, and a glass of prune juice.

Considering the production it had just taken to prepare Chuck for dinner, I asked, "Tell me about feeling terrible. What can we do about that?"

He looked at me without expression. "Nothing. I want to stop all this. But I can't. I'm their prisoner."

"You're not a prisoner. You still have some control over your life."

He raised his eyebrows, indicating he was skeptical but interested.

We sat in silence for a few minutes, both of us staring at his dinner plate.

"Do you remember about a year ago when we talked about how you could stop eating and drinking?"

He nodded. "I didn't think it would work."

"So we didn't pursue it. What do you think about that now?"

He thought a moment. "I'd like to try."

"It's your decision. Whatever you want to do, I'll support you."

After a moment, he looked up at me and said, "I'm not going to eat my dinner."

It was so Chuck. Make a decision. Implement it.

"Okay," I said, "but let's think about this for a second. We don't know if it's going to work, so why don't we wait until we've talked to Dr. Farmer. If he says it's okay, then we'll go ahead. Just eat normally tonight."

He lapsed into thought again. Finally he said, "We'll compromise. I'll eat half my dinner."

He picked up half of the roast beef sandwich, ate it, and left the other half on the plate untouched. When I asked him if he wanted me to feed him some pears, he said politely, "No, thank you."

After his half-dinner I promised to email Dr. Farmer when I got home. As I was going out the door, he said, "Now everything is right."

I turned around. "About what?"

"About my life's plan."

Then for the first time in days, he smiled.

Dr. Farmer agreed to come to St. Thomas at one o'clock the following afternoon. Though Chuck had been able to talk about his "life's plan" with me, I worried that when it came time to tell his doctor, he would forget all about it. If he did remember, would he be able to express himself? Would Dr. Farmer and Sharon accept Chuck's plan? Or would they insist he continue eating and drinking because of some arcane regulation about the care and feeding of nursing home residents? Would I be arrested as an accomplice for plotting his demise?

When I arrived at St. Thomas, I knew that Chuck was having a good day. He'd already asked his aides to dress him in clean clothes, comb his hair and beard, and transfer him to his wheelchair. Just before one o'clock, I went out into the hallway to wait for Dr. Farmer. After he arrived we asked Sharon to join us, and the three of us filed into Chuck's room. Everyone exchanged greetings, then the doctor sat on Chuck's walker and Sharon and I sat down on his bed, all three of us facing Chuck.

A few days earlier he'd been confused and unresponsive, but at this crowning moment Chuck became the teacher he had always been. He looked at us with those hazel eyes I'd always loved and began to speak.

"I want to stop all this. But I feel like a prisoner. I'm old and decrepit. I'm unproductive … I can't … do anything." His gaze dropped to his lap. I wanted to remind him again about why he was still productive. But this was Chuck's moment, so I remained silent.

"I want to stop eating and drinking." Chuck continued to stare at his lap. "That's my plan."

Dr. Farmer waited to see if he was finished before responding. "Chuck, I've known you for twenty years, and you've always been a realist. So I don't think you're depressed. I understand what you're saying and under the circumstances I might feel the same way." He said he would discontinue Chuck's medications except those for comfort and added, "I don't know if you can totally stop eating and drinking, but I'll write on your chart that you should eat and drink as much or as little as you want. How does that sound?"

Chuck lifted his gaze. "Fine."

Dr. Farmer stared into those hazel eyes. "Do you want to die?"

Without hesitating, Chuck replied, "Yes."

My heart crumpled. But he had made his decision.

The doctor suggested that we involve Hospice now, and after shaking Chuck's hand, he and Sharon left. I helped Chuck get into bed. Holding back tears, I kissed his cheek. "I'm going to go home now and call Hospice."

He looked at me and said, "Be brave."

"You mean like you?"

I will never forget the gift of his words, "Be brave." Over the past six years, Chuck had given me many gifts. It had just taken me a long time to figure out that caregiving is always, always reciprocal.

Chuck's gifts to me included his modeling of how to be brave in spite of physical and cognitive impairments—and how to live the life you've been given. He'd allowed me to be a witness to his pain and vulnerability, and he'd supplied me with ways to express my loyalty, faithfulness, and unconditional love.

My gifts to him included an advocate's voice, books read aloud by the bay, spa baths, double tall nothings, Christmas in his Santa suit, and every afternoon between 2:00 and 5:30.

Now I had only one gift left to give. I had to let him go.

# 42

# Honor Your Father

After Chuck entered Hospice, Ted and Isabel each asked if they could spend an evening with their father. Both helped Chuck eat his dinner. Then Ted wrote an email to his siblings, and Isabel wrote a poem.

*I went and saw Dad this evening and spent about an hour with him.*

*Mom has mentioned before how the staff gets Dad up for meals. Basically, this entails two aides coming into the room, waking him, changing his diaper in bed, hoisting him up, transferring him into his chair, positioning the chair and the tray table so he's in eating position, then leaving. A few minutes later a tray of food gets plopped in front of him. He then needs help getting the food and beverage from the tray into his mouth. It's all a very surreal scene, and witnessing it makes it seem even more natural that at some point a person, such as Dad, might simply say, "Don't bother."*

*He drank a cup of prune juice and a little bit of milk. He ate 1/4 of his turkey sandwich. I helped him get the straw into his mouth with the drinks but he ate the food without help (it took a long time). His eyes were kind of sealed shut with sleep gunk so it made it harder for him to know where the food was. After he ate that part of his sandwich he pushed the tray away.*

*I explained to Dad that I was there because Mom had told us his plan, and I wanted to let him know that I support his plan, and think it's a very brave thing he's decided to do and that I admired him for it. And I told him I wanted to do this now in case he was to die while I was out of town. He told me he hoped it would go quickly, but he has the feeling that he's the type of person that it will take a long time (he didn't quite muster all these words, but when I guessed what he was getting at he confirmed that I had it right).*

*I also told him that I loved him, and that he was a wonderful father to me and a wonderful grandfather to Sharky. He said, actually quite clearly, "You are a wonderful son and Sharky is a wonderful grandson." I had been thinking since last night, when I spoke to Lela about what I needed to say in order to fulfill Lela's suggestion that I "tell him everything you need to tell him." And I ended up telling him exactly that. I haven't thought of anything else that needs to be said. (I did improvise a little bit when I realized I also needed to tell him that he had a rather large piece of turkey resting on his belly.)*

*It being St. Patrick's Day, I told him some stories about my time in Ireland, and some memories of St. Patrick's Days, such as the time a homeless Irish man in Portland embraced me on the street when he learned that I was Irish, and the old man Richard in Ireland who could peg what county our Irish ancestors are from by looking at our faces.*

*That was pretty much it. I'm glad I went.*

*Love, Ted*

## LOST IN HIS MIND

*Where are you with your*
*twinkling hazel irises?*
*Windows that danced with merriment*
*now shuttered*
*Blank*
*Lost.*
*Are you hidden within this husk?*

*Your shell cracked.*
*The vitality oozed out.*

*My fingers reach out*
*brushing off crumbs.*
*Remnants of a last meal*
*litter your thick white beard.*
*Thinner now.*
*Bare patches*
*I never noticed.*

*My unspent feelings*
*are bottled inside,*
*wasted on a mind*
*that has no defense.*

*I've become the one who bore you,*
*raising quivering gelatin*
*on a dull metal spoon*
*into a mouth that does not taste.*

*What cruel irony*
*becoming the mother to the father.*

*Is that still you?*
*Are you in there?*
*I do not want this duty*
*I cannot refuse.*

*Was that a spark of your soul*
*I saw in your eyes*
*just then?*
*Was that a forgotten twinkle?*
*Or a trick of the light*
*giving birth to a momentary hope*
*just as quickly dying.*

*I sigh softly,*
*and reach out once more*
*to brush crumbs*
*from a well-known unfamiliar face.*

—Isabel Anne Munat Cole

# 43

# Shiva the Destroyer

Hospice generally admits people who are expected to live six months or less.

When Chuck entered Hospice, none of us knew if his plan to reduce his eating and drinking and to stop his medications would bring about his death in six months or six years. Technically, he did not have a terminal illness. But he had expressed his wish to let go of his life. Would his determination be enough to bring about his death?

Chuck entered Hospice ten days before my birthday, and Ted asked six-year-old Sharky what they should buy me for a present. After that Christmas in the stairwell with Papa, Sharky had been diagnosed with autism. But since then, he had been making steady gains in socialization and learning. He had become a companionable, loving little boy who was now achieving at grade level in the Seattle public schools.

Sharky answered Ted's question without hesitation, "A red monkey with a blue heart." Father and son drove to a local toy store where they found a stuffed monkey of that description. At least, it was a mostly red monkey with a blue tail, a blue and white striped leg, blue hands, and a cream-colored face with a kind smile. I told a friend, "They actually found me a red monkey! It doesn't have a blue heart, but that's okay."

And my friend, who's been a special education teacher for many years, replied, "How do you know? The heart is on the inside. Sharky knows the monkey's heart is blue." Of course he did. Because he knew mine was. Sharky told me that the monkey's name was George Abberson. George now sits atop the red pillows on my bed.

Chuck's Hospice nurse was a tall blond woman named Elaine. She had just started her job the week before, and Chuck was her first patient. That fact was a bit unsettling, but any doubts about her experience were dispelled by Elaine's competency, confidence, and caring. Each time she visited St. Thomas, she would kneel down next to Chuck's bed, take his hand, and, *sotto voce*, tell him her name and ask if it was all right to begin her ministrations. Following the pattern of LBD roller-coaster fluctuations, Chuck would sometimes open his eyes and brightly greet her; other times he would not move or speak. Elaine told me more than once, "Just when I think I've got Chuck pegged, he surprises me. He's teaching me patience and not to jump to conclusions."

*Sharky, who knew that I needed a red monkey with a blue heart.*

Days went by, and then weeks. A few times when I entered his room, I found him dressed and sitting in his wheelchair eating lunch. God forgive me, but at those moments my first thought was, *Are we going to do this for another six years?* Sometimes the aides would tell me he'd eaten his entire breakfast. When I reminded him of his "life's plan," he would say, "I remember." End of discussion.

Both Dr. Farmer and Elaine told me that it didn't matter how much Chuck ate or didn't eat. I think they were telling me that the dying process had begun.

Chuck's longstanding masseuse Clare continued to provide his weekly massages. I think her blindness helped her intuit the exact length and intensity Chuck needed for each session. Her reports about his energy fields and physical responses to her massages provided invaluable information to his Hospice team.

Many people from Hospice stopped by Chuck's room on a regular basis: his nurse Elaine, his bath aide, the social worker, the chaplain, and his Hospice volunteer. Each time, it felt like angels had drifted into the room. They took over much of the decision-making for Chuck's care, which lifted a huge burden from my heart. They answered my questions, calmed my fears, and brought the nursing home staff on board regarding changes in Chuck's medications and food. I don't know how I could have gone through that period without their loving care of Chuck—and me.

But there were many hours I waited alone in Chuck's room, sitting with him while he slept. He no longer watched television or wanted me to read to him. I lacked the concentration to read a book, so I draped myself over the arm of his recliner and spent hours playing Klondike solitaire on my handheld device. I noted any changes in his breathing or whether his occasional groans might indicate pain or hunger—or nothing in particular. I came to the facility at lunch and dinnertime to see what he ate. Before Chuck entered Hospice, when I left for the day I'd always said, "See you tomorrow." But now when I left, I didn't know if I would see him again. So I just said, "See you soon."

In mid-April, I searched for a 75th birthday card with an appropriate message. I finally bought one that said, "With wishes for today and love for always." I never gave it to him. By the time his birthday arrived, on 25 April 2009, Chuck would not have known what the words meant or even what a card was. And the days following weren't much different.

Two months had passed since his admission to Hospice. Chuck spent most days in bed. Sometimes he spoke; sometimes he was silent. When his legs hurt, the hall nurse administered pain medication, as per Hospice. He slept more but no longer cried out. His food intake definitely decreased, but I fed him if he indicated he was hungry. Sugar-free popsicles kept his mouth moist and he always seemed to love them, so I kept a couple boxes in the nursing home freezer.

One afternoon I was sitting in a chair next to his bedside holding his hand while he slept. The gravity of this part of our journey was now weighing heavily on me. I'd just laid my cheek on the blanket when I felt him squeeze my hand. I looked up, but he still appeared to be asleep. I thought about the infinite number of touches we'd shared during our marriage, and I knew this was one of the sweetest.

One evening in May, I was sitting at home leafing through the newspaper's travel section when I came across an advertisement for the *Clipper*, the fast boat that ferries people between Seattle and Victoria, B.C. According to the ad, $300 bought you a round-trip on the *Clipper* and three nights in a Victoria hotel near the Inner Harbour. Suddenly gripped by an intense desire to get away, I went online and checked it out. I entered all my booking information and selected a mid-priced hotel a few blocks from the *Clipper* terminal and one block from Parliament. Then I typed in my credit card information. But when it came time to click the "Book This Trip" button, I balked.

*I'm booking a trip? What kind of person goes on vacation when her husband is dying?*

Maybe an emotionally drained person? A person who needs a few days away so she can return with renewed energy? I told myself these things, but I still couldn't hit the button. I phoned Ted and explained. "Would you please tell me it's okay to hit the 'Book This Trip' button?"

"Hit the button," he said. "Hit the button with my full blessing."

I hit the button.

A few days later as I was rolling my suitcase along the Seattle waterfront to the *Clipper* terminal, my cell phone rang. When I saw that Elaine was the caller, I thought, *He's dead. At least I haven't boarded the boat.*

But she had called to say that she'd stopped by Chuck's room to deliver some medical supplies. He'd been sleeping, but his eyes popped open when she whispered, "Chuck, it's Elaine."

He'd barely spoken in the last few days, so you can imagine her surprise when he looked at her and casually said, "Oh, hi, Elaine."

She asked if she could get him anything.

"A cup of coffee?" he said.

She queried, "And how do you take your coffee?"

"Black," he said, which was the way he always ordered it, often adding, "Black and bitter, like life."

So they shared a cup of coffee, and she was calling to wish me well on my trip. She thought his cognition was amazing, considering what she'd observed recently. I told her, "Welcome to the world of Lewy body dementia, land of fluctuations."

If there exists a Great Travel Agent in the Sky, she must have tailor-made my trip to Victoria. On my first day, I strolled through the spectacular Butchart Gardens with hundreds of other tourists. Along the pathways, I heard people speaking French, Chinese, Greek, Russian, Japanese, Spanish, and other languages I couldn't identify. On the bus ride back to my hotel, I sat next to two couples exchanging comments in animated Italian.

The next day at the Royal British Columbia Museum, I toured the gallery of a traveling exhibit from the British Museum called "Treasures." The exhibit was composed of relics and artifacts from every continent and all eras of world history. The first object I saw was a stone hand axe carved between 1.6 and 1.4 million years ago in Tanzania's Olduvai Gorge. Other exhibits that intrigued me were a gold death mask made in Jerusalem in the first century A.D., a Chaucer astrolabe from fifteenth-century England, and five chess pieces made of walrus ivory from the Outer Hebrides in Scotland around 1150 A.D. Given our love for New Zealand, I was especially pleased to see a Maori meeting house lintel carved in the Bay of Islands in 1840.

As I walked through the Asia Gallery, a docent approached me carrying a small black iron statue. "Would you like to hold this?" she asked. "It's 200 years old, and one of the only items we allow people to handle. It's from India."

I took the figure and cupped it in my hands, feeling its heft and its mystery.

She continued, "This is Shiva, one of the major Hindu deities. Shiva is the Destroyer. All matter is destroyed. But he is also the Preserver, for as quickly as life is destroyed, it is preserved in new forms. A constant recycling."

Before this trip to Victoria, I'd been focused on my own small space on this small planet—and my own small drama being played out in a nursing home on an island in Puget Sound. And rightly so. That was my role at that moment in time, and I was honoring my responsibility and my deep desire to usher my husband and myself through his last journey.

But it was good to be reminded that for millions of years, millions of people have lived and died on this earth. My drama was not unique, and in a way, that made it easier to bear. Shiva the Destroyer is Shiva the Preserver. How can something that is destroyed also be preserved? I don't understand this. But I do believe it. Remember, I held that mystery in my hands.

# 44

# See You Soon

Chuck died on Saturday, June 6, 2009, at 9:00 p.m. at St. Thomas Health & Rehabilitation Center, less than three months after he told me to "be brave" and entered Hospice.

For six years his life had been a series of "lasts." The last time he drove his car. Last time he read the sports section. Last time he used a walker. Last time he went outside and felt the sun on his face. Last time he talked. On the last evening, it was just Chuck in his bed, eyes closed, free of pain, silent.

I had been summoned to his bedside at 4:30 a.m. that Friday. For six years I had slept with both my cell phone and landline phone on my bedside table in case I got "The call." On June 5, I finally got it. I drove to St. Thomas where I gave Chuck's feverish body a cool sponge bath. Then I pushed the recliner next to his bed and waited.

Elaine came, and though Chuck wasn't responsive, she spoke to him because she said that hearing is the last sense to go. She thanked him for all he had taught her about patience and the hard work of dying. She said she would never forget him, her first Hospice patient. Her words brought tears to my eyes. I thanked her for treating Chuck with the dignity and admiration he deserved. She gently told me that she expected him to go in twenty-four to forty-eight hours.

Ted arrived, and he and I sat in the gazebo behind the nursing home while he called his siblings to let them know. I had only been able to manage the one phone call to him.

Word spread, and friends and family came and went. I spent much of the last two days in Chuck's room, stroking him, telling him how much I loved him and how proud I was of him. We played Irish folk music on his boom box and kept cool cloths on his warm body. We sprayed his dry mouth with water from an atomizer.

On Saturday evening I came back to the condo with my children and grandchildren and served them dinner—a meal brought to me precooked by my thoughtful friend Nancy. Ted made a cocktail punch, and we stood around the punch bowl on the kitchen counter, sipping and talking. Ben and Kate, having just arrived from Portland, left for the nursing home. I asked them to let me know if anything had changed since that afternoon.

Isabel and James and Alex departed on the 8:55 p.m. ferry. They said it would not be necessary for them to return; they had already said their good-byes.

At nine o'clock as I watched their ferry sail out of the harbor, Ben called from St. Thomas to say, "He's gone."

Ted and I drove over to the nursing home and joined Ben and Kate in Room 30. We each took a little time to be alone with Chuck. I slipped his wedding ring off his finger and put it on my thumb; later I would wear it on a silver chain around my neck, as I'd once worn his driftwood creations.

When the four of us reconvened in Chuck's room, we shared some of our final words. "You did it." "Good job." "I love you so much. See you soon."

Of course, there had to be an element of absurdity. Otherwise, it wouldn't have been consistent with what I'd come to expect from the nursing home.

Tedi, the hall nurse, was a woman I'd never seen before. She told me she was required to report Chuck's death to the county coroner. She had no experience doing this, so I thought I should stay with her. As I stood in the hallway next to her nursing cart, I could only hear her end of the phone conversation. Apparently the man from the coroner's office was giving her a hard time.

She said, "Sir, I'm trying to work with you on this, you don't have to be so rude."

When he asked her the cause of death, she turned and queried me. I didn't know what to say. One doesn't actually die of Lewy body dementia, and that raised the question of how he did die. Should we go for the all-inclusive "cardiac arrest"?

Tedi sent an aide to retrieve Chuck's chart. The aide ran back to us and handed Tedi the loose-leaf book, which after six years was approaching encyclopedic size and weight. She set it on the cart and leafed through the pages while speaking into the phone, citing every condition Chuck had experienced in the past six years: aphasia, insomnia, diabetes, stomach flu, etc.

Finally, I suggested to Tedi, "Just say he died of complications from Lewy body dementia." That seemed to be acceptable.

A few weeks later, I received copies of Chuck's death certificate. Dr. Farmer had described the cause of death with this medical and poetic description: "Failure to thrive."

# 45

# Thin Times

Celtic wisdom speaks of *thin places*—specific geographic locations like the island of Iona in Scotland. These are said to be sacred sites where the veil between earth and heaven, or life and death, is a sheer, fluttering fabric—and where one can perhaps experience the Divine.

Others speak of *thin times*, which can occur after the death of a loved one. During thin times, deep truths may be revealed while you are momentarily balanced on the threshold between life and death. After Chuck died, I wanted to be quiet and pay attention because I thought I might be going through such liminal thin times.

Father's Day arrived two weeks after Chuck's death. I awoke that morning at five o'clock, fell back to sleep, and dreamed this dream.

I had driven Chuck into the mountains of a national park where wildflowers grew in verdant meadows. It resembled Hurricane Ridge, the area of Olympic National Park that he and I had loved. When my dream began, Chuck had already hiked off into the meadows, and I was left behind at a rustic lodge. I was standing among a bunch of noisy tourists sitting at picnic tables. I glanced around hoping to find Chuck, but I knew he'd left me.

My cell phone rang. When I pulled it from my pocket, I saw that it wasn't my phone but a device that looked like Chuck's simplified TV remote control. However, it was ringing so I answered—and it was Chuck. He urged me to join him so I could see what he was seeing, which was very beautiful. I told him he'd gotten a head start, and I wouldn't be able to catch up. He continued to encourage me to come.

This conversation repeated itself several times until finally he said, "I didn't say you would see me. I just said you should come. It's so beautiful! You can see the Olympics."

Was he reassuring me that he's in a beautiful place? Was he telling me to embrace the rest of my journey on earth? Was I giving myself permission to go on with my life?

Or was it simply a dream?

# 46

# To Remember and Celebrate the Life of Chuck Munat

The above words are printed on each page of the program handed out at Chuck's memorial service, which was held at Grace Church at his request. They are good words. Yes, of course we wanted to celebrate his life. It was a good life once he got beyond a difficult boyhood. He was a journalist, a birder, a dreamer, a warrior, an editor and writer, a lover, a father, a husband, a genealogist, an activist, and above all, a teacher. So we celebrated that. We remembered the good stories.

Our sister-in-law Clare came from Vermont. James flew all the way from New Zealand. Our friend Pipper designed floral arrangements for the church using wildflowers that Chuck loved. The rainbow PEACE flag that Chuck's sister Judith had given him hung from the altar.

*Grace Church on the day of Chuck's memorial service,*
*with his PACE (Italian for PEACE) flag hanging from the altar.*

During the service, my college friend Sarah read the eulogy I'd written for Chuck, and added her own recollections of meeting him in Chicago in the late 1960s. James spoke warmly of his AFS dad, shared memories of his Middletown days, and told how much his three children loved receiving the huge mailbags filled with books that Chuck sent them every few months. Isabel recited poems she'd written about her father, including one about Chuck teaching her to ride a bicycle in Chicago. Alex read her Obama Inauguration article. Ted read a letter he'd written to Chuck on Father's Day 2008, telling him how much Papa meant to Sharky. In between speeches, we sang some of Chuck's favorite songs: "We Shall Overcome," "Amazing Grace," "Turn, Turn, Turn," "When the Saints Go Marching In," and "Peace Like a River."

The minister spoke of Chuck's generosity. He said that Chuck had spent an enormous amount of time giving of himself to others, and therefore his life had infinite value. The love Chuck had brought to the world would continue to live on in us.

For the reception in the church hall, the caterer made tiny ham and pineapple pizzas. Ben and Charles organized photos of Chuck into a slide show that displayed on a big-screen TV in a corner of the hall. Ted and Ben ripped more than a hundred CDs with music from the civil rights era, and we gave one to each person as a gift of remembrance.

But once the celebrating was over, we were left with the grieving. We'd been grieving Chuck throughout his illness. Yet after his death, our feelings were as raw as if we'd had no preparation at all.

Grief does not feel like celebration. Sometimes it feels like heaviness in your limbs. Sometimes it robs you of your will to get out of bed in the morning. Grief comes and goes like winter fog. You could be pushing your grocery cart through the cereal aisle when someone asks, "How are you?" And those words send you dashing for the parking lot with tears in your eyes and a lost feeling in your heart.

Any honest philosophy of life must admit the presence of mystery—the acknowledgment that parts of our lives cannot be explained or comprehended. For me, that mystery now wraps around certain questions. Why did a ten-month-old baby die on the operating table? Why did a vibrant, young dancer like Carol succumb to pneumonia? Why did Chuck have to go, and I have to stay?

Not long after Chuck died, I watched a movie in which a mother is dying of cancer. She calls her young son to her deathbed and instructs him, "You best not be sad. Promise?" Then she tells her friend not to bring the boy to her funeral.

Don't be sad? What terrible advice! By asking her son to deny his sorrow, she is asking him to deny his love—and therefore, his humanity. Because make no mistake: when human beings love and lose, they grieve.

Does grieving make us better or stronger? If we push through it, will we feel better? Certainly, grieving marks our souls with a searing intensity. Just as external scars indicate where our bodies have been torn, sorrow creates internal scars.

One night when I was five years old, I tripped over a metal toy truck and cut my shin. My parents drove me to the emergency room where it took eleven stitches to close the wound. A week later, my pediatrician took out the stitches slowly and agonizingly—the way doctors had to do in those days. He somberly pondered the half-moon scar on my leg, raised his eyes to look at me, and nodded. "You're going to have that scar for a long, long time," he said.

Six decades later, I still have that half-moon scar on my leg. What are the odds I will ever lose my internal scars, the ones I bear from having lost the love of my life?

The good news is: I don't want to lose them. That sorrow is a part of who I am now, a part of my mysterious journey. And contrary to everything I once believed, I wouldn't change it if I could.

Wherever I find love in my life now, I know Chuck is there.

*The bay in Akaroa, New Zealand,*
*where I scattered Chuck's ashes.*